Larousse
Best Desserts Ever

Larousse
Best Desserts Ever

Larousse and Co., Inc.,
New York

Librairie Larousse thanks *le Centre d'etudes et de documentation du sucre* who have collected the illustrations and perfected the chosen recipes for this book following the suggestions of Marie-Paule Bernardin.

The photographs are by Mireille Bianquis, Max Danton, Jacques Masson, Henri Yeru, and Thérèse Zadora.

Originally published by Librairie Larousse, Paris under the title
LES 100 MEILLEURS DESSERTS
© Copyright Librairie Larousse 1977
© Copyright English text The Hamlyn Publishing Group Limited 1979
First published in the United States in 1979 by
Larousse and Co., Inc.
572 Fifth Avenue
New York, N.Y. 10036

Third impression 1983

ISBN 0-88332-115-7
LOC Catalog Card No 78-74630
Printed in Hong Kong

Contents

Useful Facts and Figures

Notes on metrication

Exact conversion from Imperial to metric measures does not usually give very convenient working quantities and so the metric measures have been rounded off into units of 25 grams. The table below shows the recommended equivalents.

Ounces	Approx g to nearest whole figure	Recommended conversion to nearest unit of 25
1	28	25
2	57	50
3	85	75
4	113	100
5	142	150
6	170	175
7	198	200
8	227	225
9	255	250
10	283	275
11	312	300
12	340	350
13	368	375
14	396	400
15	425	425
16 (1 lb)	454	450
17	482	475
18	510	500
19	539	550
20 ($1\frac{1}{4}$ lb)	567	575

Note: When converting quantities over 20 oz first add the appropriate figures in the centre column, then adjust to the nearest unit of 25. As a general guide, 1 kg (1000 g) equals 2.2 lb or about 2 lb 3 oz. This method of conversion gives good results in nearly all cases, although in certain pastry and cake recipes a more accurate conversion is necessary to produce a balanced recipe.

Liquid measures The millilitre has been used in this book and the following table gives a few examples.

Imperial	Approx ml to nearest whole figure	Recommended ml
$\frac{1}{4}$ pint	142	150 ml
$\frac{1}{2}$ pint	283	300 ml
$\frac{3}{4}$ pint	425	450 ml
1 pint	567	600 ml
$1\frac{1}{2}$ pints	851	900 ml
$1\frac{3}{4}$ pints	992	1000 ml (1 litre)

Spoon measures All spoon measures given in this book are level unless otherwise stated.

Can sizes At present, cans are marked with the exact (usually to the nearest whole number) metric equivalent of the Imperial weight of the contents, so we have followed this practice when giving can sizes.

Oven temperatures

The table below gives recommended equivalents.

	°C	°F	Gas Mark
Very cool	110	225	$\frac{1}{4}$
	120	250	$\frac{1}{2}$
Cool	140	275	1
	150	300	2
Moderate	160	325	3
	180	350	4
Moderately hot	190	375	5
	200	400	6
Hot	220	425	7
	230	450	8
Very hot	240	475	9

Notes for American and Australian users

In American the 8-oz measuring cup is used. In Australia metric measures are now used in conjunction with the standard 250-ml measuring cup. The Imperial pint, used in Britain and Australia, is 20 fl oz, while the American pint is 16 fl oz. It is important to remember that the Australian tablespoon differs from both the British and American tablespoons; the table below gives a comparison. The British standard tablespoon, which has been used throughout this book, holds 17.7 ml, the American 14.2 ml, and the Australian 20 ml. A teaspoon holds approximately 5 ml in all three countries.

British	American	Australian
1 teaspoon	1 teaspoon	1 teaspoon
1 tablespoon	1 tablespoon	1 tablespoon
2 tablespoons	3 tablespoons	2 tablespoons
$3\frac{1}{2}$ tablespoons	4 tablespoons	3 tablespoons
4 tablespoons	5 tablespoons	$3\frac{1}{2}$ tablespoons

Note: WHEN MAKING ANY OF THE RECIPES IN THIS BOOK, ONLY FOLLOW ONE SET OF MEASURES AS THEY ARE NOT INTERCHANGEABLE.

American terms

The list below gives some American equivalents or substitutes for equipment, terms and ingredients used in this book.

British	American
Equipment and terms	
baked/unbaked pastry case	baked/unbaked pie shell
cake mixture	cake batter
cocktail stick	toothpick
deep cake tin	springform pan
flan	open or single crusted pie
flan ring/tin	pie pan
greaseproof paper	waxed paper
icing/piping bag	pastry bag
knob of butter	nut of butter
liquidiser	blender
knock back	punch down
packet	package
palette knife	spatula
pinch	dash
sachet	envelope
sandwich tin	layer cake pan
star nozzle	fluted nozzle/tip
stoned	pitted
Swiss roll tin	jelly roll pan
tart	double crusted pie
Ingredients	
bilberries	blueberries
black cherries	Bing cherries
broad bean	lima or fava bean
castor sugar	granulated or superfine sugar
cornflour	cornstarch
demerara sugar	soft brown sugar
double cream	heavy cream
dried yeast	active dry yeast
essence	extract
glacé cherries	candied cherries
icing sugar	confectioners' sugar
mandarins	tangerines
pastry	dough
potato flour	potato starch
single cream	light cream
sponge fingers	lady fingers
vanilla pod	vanilla bean

Introduction

One hundred desserts . . . One hundred desserts assured of success, from the most simple to the most elaborate, one hundred moments of happiness to end a meal: such is the aim of this book with its hundred mouthwatering photographs, each, of course, with a clear, detailed recipe to accompany it.

But that is not all. The present work also includes the basic principles of home baking, the tricks of the trade and steps to making successful cakes, tarts and creams, thanks to the accumulated experience of housewives eager to round off a meal with the reward that a dessert always gives, a reward for both the eater and the cook.

New ideas too, due to better materials and more trustworthy cooking equipment, have allowed an up-to-date perfecting of old skills.

Furthermore you can concoct variations on the dishes or simplify or enrich a basic recipe according to the time available or the occasion to be celebrated.

One hundred desserts is a lot, but it is little compared with the thousands of recipes that could be included. Then why choose these hundred? Firstly there are recipes that it was only reasonable to choose, classic or traditional recipes that it is essential to know, explained in the best possible way and ranging from a wholesome fruit sponge to heavenly chocolate mousse. Then after some exploration of regional dishes we have wandered further afield and included unexpected recipes, chosen because at some time they gave great pleasure to someone who tasted them.

They are desserts then, chosen for the pleasure of giving pleasure. One hundred? Because there are at least a hundred times during the year when you will wish to round off a meal with a small celebration. With all the information collected in this book seasonal and festive dishes become easy to make, from pancakes for Shrove Tuesday to the unvarying but so versatile Christmas log and the beautiful fresh fruit tarts of country holidays.

Here is a joy in living which is typically French and which will allow you to enjoy to the full the occasions when the family is reunited, when you have the opportunity to entertain friends or to honour your guests. It is a rich dessert which comes straight from the kitchen, heartily enjoyed and justifying the feeling shared by all though rarely expressed – yes, it is true, happiness lies in a little greediness!

Dessert ingredients

Even the most sumptuous and elaborate desserts require only the simplest, most basic food products, those which every cook always has to hand: flour and milk, eggs and butter, sugar and fruit and also a few flavourings such as chocolate, coffee, vanilla . . . It is only necessary to choose good quality products and to adopt the best method in order to be successful.

It is something like the alphabet which allows man to compose the whole of literature, or like the ten numerals which make up the scientific calculations which have led man into space: the mixing of these few basic products, provided that the best method is used and the recipe is closely followed, is sufficient to create delightful dishes.

Cereals, flour and flour products

The use of cereals and in particular the use of flour obtained by grinding grain dates from earliest times. Nowadays wheat flour is predominantly used, but other products derived from corn (such as semolina), maize flour and maize starch, and rice play an important part in the preparation of desserts. It is therefore necessary to know how to choose them and to learn to use them.

Flour

Since it keeps for a relatively short time (a few months) there is no point in bulk buying. Avoid damp places and store in an airtight container.

Flour derived from wheat should be a creamy white in colour, soft to the touch and with a pleasant smell. For layered pastry, brioches and all bread making choose a strong flour which is high in gluten.
Buckwheat or Saracen corn is used especially for some regional dishes, such as Breton pancakes.
Maize flour (U.S. cornmeal), which is more yellow in colour than wheat flour, is chosen for certain regional or foreign dishes.

Hints on use
• Too much flour produces a hard-textured pastry, making it dry and difficult to handle.
• Always sift flour before use, particularly when it is to be

11

added to a mixture all at once. This will avoid uneven distribution of flour.

Do not continually sprinkle a pastry board with flour on the pretext that the pastry is sticky. This will alter the proportions and you risk ending up with a tart or cake which is inedible. The flour on the board should merely absorb any excess moisture in the pastry so very little is needed. The rolling pin and pastry should be lightly handled. Turn the pastry on the board frequently.

Starch

Edible starch, which is extremely finely grained, is white and powdery in appearance. It is therefore perfect for thickening, but pastries made with starch, such as corn-flour and rice flour, although lighter are also shorter than an all-flour pastry.

Nevertheless, some recipes recommend replacing part of the flour with starch to make it lighter.
Potato flour is white and shiny and crackly to the touch. *Maize starch*, more commonly known as cornflour (u.s. corn starch), is used for light, delicate recipes, fine pastries and creams where it gives excellent results.

There are also other starches such as crème de riz or pure ground rice.

Hints on use
Always dilute the starch in a little cold liquid before adding to a cream or a hot liquid.
• Stir continuously until it thickens.
• All creams made with flour or starch will thicken on cooling.

Semolina

This is a cereal product, mostly wheat, reduced by coarse milling to a granular texture which is much coarser than flour. Semolina is available in several different grain textures.

Hints on use
Semolina can be used to make puddings, sweets and family desserts which while economical will be enjoyed by the children.
• Always sprinkle the semolina on to milk or other liquids while boiling.
• Do not add sugar until cooked.

Tapioca

This is obtained by treating the starch which is extracted from manioc roots. It has the essential characteristics of being extremely digestible and a perfect thickening material if used correctly. It can make a mixture thick and smooth and is used for creams, sweets, cakes and milk puddings.

Hints on use
• Always sprinkle on to boiling liquid and stir with a wooden spoon until it thickens.
• Do not add sugar until cooked.

Rice

This is a graminaceous grain which undergoes various processes such as bleaching and polishing before being sold in the form in which we know it. The different types of rice are distinguished by the shape of the grains, more or less round or more or less long. Round-grain rice is best for desserts.

One also finds varieties of rice prepared in different ways:
• Basic, loose, white rice is the cheapest and in the long run the easiest to use when one knows exactly how to cook it.
• American rice is golden yellow in colour. It takes longer to cook than the usual bleached rice, but the grains will not stick together.
• For pre-cooked rice, which has already been partially cooked, follow the cooking times indicated on the packet.

Hints on use
• Wash the rice under the tap in a colander, but do not soak it.
• Do not mix remains of different varieties which have different cooking times.
• For easier cooking of rice in milk, blanch the rice for 1 minute in a little boiling water, then finish cooking in boiling milk. The slower the cooking in the milk, the better will be the results.
• Do not add sugar until cooked. To avoid damaging the grains mix the sugar carefully with a fork.

Milk and cream

Milk and milk products play an important part in the making of desserts and particularly in the case of creams and sweets. They increase the nutritional value of the dessert and are often the only source of milk in the diet of those who do not like its taste. Nowadays it is rare to find milk in its natural state; almost all fresh milk is heat treated to destroy harmful bacteria and increase its keeping qualities. This includes pasteurisation, sterilising and ultra heat treatment.

Milk

Untreated milk should always be boiled before use. Other milks, pasteurised, sterilised, homogenised or long-life, can all be used interchangeably in desserts.

Evaporated or powdered milks, from which part or all

of the water has been removed, should have water added following the manufacturer's instructions if they are then to be used as a normal milk.

Milks containing little animal fat can also be used to make certain desserts, particularly for people who are following a diet. However, avoid fat-free milks which could cause some recipes to fail. Everything depends on the role that milk plays in the recipe.

Cream

Fresh cream, either natural or whipped, is often used in making desserts. It is used for ice creams, especially if you are not using an ice cream maker, for it helps to prevent ice crystals forming. Use double cream (u.s. heavy cream) for whipping as single cream (u.s. light cream) will not thicken. When buying cream, check the date code and always refrigerate as it deteriorates quickly.

Butter and other fats

Butter, which in the mind of the eater is synonymous with good pastries, is widely used for desserts, and in particular for pastry. It is important to choose a very fresh, good quality butter. Sometimes for economy or in particular recipes another type of fat may be preferable; oil for fried dishes for example, or the fat of various animals for regional recipes.

Choosing butter

There are two types of butter: Sweet Cream (either salted or unsalted) and Lactic (either slightly salted or un-salted). The important point in pastry making is to use a fresh butter with no rancid taste which would be evident when eaten. With the exception of some regional dishes, it is preferable to use unsalted or slightly salted butter in pastry making.

Hints on use
• It is best to take butter out of the refrigerator shortly before you use it (the time will vary with the time of year) so that it will not be too hard. If, on the contrary, the butter is too soft and sticks to the wrapper, you should stand it for a few minutes in cold water containing a few ice cubes and it will firm up sufficiently.
• To melt butter for a recipe, cut it into small pieces and place in a pan over a low heat so that it melts completely at the same time.
• To cream butter, beat the butter which should be quite soft with a wooden spoon, or if necessary with an electric mixer using the beaters, but never heat it.
• To grease a tin you can heat the tin and coat it with a lump of butter which will be melted by the heat of the tin. You can also brush it with butter which is just melted.

Oil

Choose a good quality oil. Ground-nut oil with its sweet flavour is used most often for desserts.

Other fats

Margarine is often used for cake and pastry making. It is made from vegetable and/or animal fats, except for certain brands which contain only vegetable oils. For pastry making it is better to use a firm margarine. Sometimes in recipes which need a lot of butter one can use half butter, half margarine.

Eggs

Eggs are of prime importance in sweets and pastries for they are a good binding agent and give a characteristic smoothness, whether used in small or large quantities, whole or separated. Yolks can be used on their own and the whites can be stiffly whisked.

Depending on the desired end product each recipe uses

The egg white is almost entirely made up of albumen. Bubbles of air can be incorporated into it by whisking until stiff. These air bubbles must remain intact when the white is folded into the other ingredients. During cooking the heat causes the air to expand and the whole cake will rise. The albumen coagulates and hardens: the cake is then set at its maximum size and if the coagulation is complete it will not collapse afterwards. This is why it is usual to test if a cake is cooked by piercing the centre, the part which takes longest to cook, with a skewer: if the skewer comes out clean, the cake is cooked. Do not open the oven door during the initial cooking as the cake may sink as the cold air enters the oven.

Choosing eggs

A fresh egg should have a rounded, shiny yolk and a white which should be sticky rather than runny and difficult to separate from the yolk. The air pocket should be small and shallow. Eggs are sorted according to size.

It is obligatory to mark the packing with the size (which indicates the weight) of the eggs. With the exception of particular cases where the quantity of eggs in the recipe is measured exactly, as for example in choux pastry where it corresponds to the weight of a medium egg (55 g/2 oz), it is best to choose large eggs, as cakes and soufflés will rise better the larger the eggs.

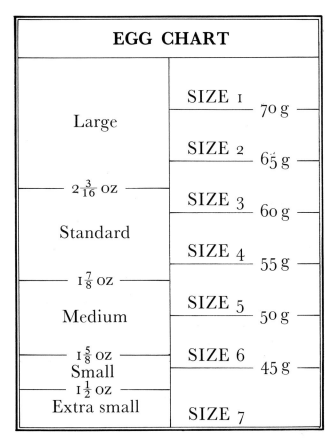

EGG CHART		
Large	SIZE 1	70 g
	SIZE 2	65 g
2 3/16 oz	SIZE 3	60 g
Standard	SIZE 4	55 g
1 7/8 oz	SIZE 5	50 g
Medium	SIZE 6	45 g
1 5/8 oz		
Small		
1 1/2 oz		
Extra small	SIZE 7	

the particular properties of the yolk and white of the egg.

The protein in the yolk will coagulate at about 80°C/156°F and become hard. That is why custard which has been heated beyond the coagulating temperature will separate and also explains why an omelette which has been cooked for a short time only is 'runny'.

The fats which are naturally emulsified in the yolk, that is they are divided into an infinite number of particles, can act as an emulsifier on other fats, as in butter cream or chocolate marchioness (see page 110).

Hints on use

● If eggs are kept in the refrigerator, preferably standing on the pointed end, take them out about 1 hour before using them.

● Always break eggs separately so that one egg which may be bad will not spoil the rest.

● Avoid contact with silver spoons or other silver items which will readily tarnish.

● Separate eggs very carefully, for the smallest particle of yolk in the whites will prevent them from incorporating air. To beat whites you can use either a hand or electric whisk, but be sure to choose a clean, grease-free bowl large enough to allow for the increase in bulk.

● Do not whisk egg whites until just before you are ready to add them to the mixture. Take care when mixing whites into a dish; in almost all recipes they will be added last. If the mixture is a bit thick use one spoon of the beaten whites and stir in vigorously to make softer. Then, touching it as little as possible, place the rest of the whites on to the mixture and fold in carefully with a metal spoon until well incorporated into the mixture. When the mixture is uniform pour the mixture in a stream into the tin.

Sugar

Without it there can be no dessert! The sweet taste is essentially that which nowadays distinguishes between a dessert and other dishes. There are several forms of sugar. If every recipe is to be a perfect success one must choose the type of sugar which suits it best and learn to add it in the right way and at the right time.

Castor sugar is a granular powder most often used for desserts as it dissolves quickly. It is used for cakes, pastries (especially in an egg mixture), for creams, fruit salads, meringues and to sweeten fritters and pancakes when cooked.

● To add sugar to egg yolks, sprinkle on to the eggs, stirring slowly at first then more quickly. If poured in all at once it is slower to dissolve and the mixture would take longer to become pale, frothy and double in volume, as it should.

● Added to pastry, sugar will help it to brown in cooking and will make it more crisp: this is what happens in rubbed-in pastry or pancake batter.

● It is best to sweeten stewed fruit, rice dishes, semolina or tapioca when cooked.

Cube sugar is recommended for a successful caramel and more generally for all forms of sugar syrup. It is enough to place each cube under the tap to moisten it. It is also practical to use cube sugar if you have no kitchen scales:

    1 small cube weighs 2 grams.
    1 average cube weighs 4 grams.

Granulated sugar is coarser than castor sugar, but can be used if you have no castor sugar. It is less expensive but dissolves more slowly. Granulated sugar is used for fruit pies and to decorate some cakes. If used to sugar a greased tin, it will help to prevent the cake sticking to the tin.

In America, granulated sugar is of a finer grain than that used in Britain and can be used in most recipes calling for either granulated or castor sugar. However, it is recommended that American superfine sugar is used with uncooked fruits as it dissolves more rapidly.

Icing sugar (U.S. confectioners' sugar) is a fine powdered sugar which must be protected from damp. It is therefore best not to buy large quantities and to keep it dry in an airtight container.

Icing sugar is used for icing and decorating cakes, and is recommended for making ice creams and sorbets.

It also ensures more success when whipping crème Chantilly.

Demerara sugar is a raw cane sugar with a taste similar to that of rum.

15

Soft brown sugar is a brown sugar from cane or beet which is partly refined and may be preferred for some traditional recipes. However, if a recipe indicates the use of one of these sugars and you do not have it, it can always be replaced by castor sugar.

Fruits

One could say that almost all fruits will be used at some time in a dessert.

Fresh fruit

Some fresh fruits can be found all year round, and the present-day international markets have tended to make the seasons disappear; however fruits are always best and least expensive at the height of their season.
● Citrus fruits, which include lemons, oranges, grapefruits, mandarins and clementines, are sold almost throughout the year, but they are best and cheapest in winter.

The peels are used for flavouring (take care to choose for

this purpose fruits with untreated skins) and the whole fruit for salads, pies and cakes.

They are also used for frosted fruits (sorbets served in the fruit itself).
● Bananas and pineapples, also found all year round, are easy to obtain. Pineapples, which were once a rare and luxury food, are now used in many desserts or may be served alone with crème Chantilly.
● Grapes – blue, black, red, amber and green – are available all year round.
● Soft fruits such as currants, strawberries and raspberries are summer and autumn fruit. They are very delicate and must be used quickly and without too much handling, which is why they are often used uncooked on tarts or to decorate cakes. They also make excellent fresh fruit salads.
● Apples are all year round fruit, but the varieties differ according to the season and country of origin. Bramley's Seedling is one variety recommended for cooking.

Peaches, apricots, nectarines and pears have many uses: tarts, stewed fruit, charlottes, salads, decorating cakes, sorbets . . .

Nowadays a great variety of new fruits are available from abroad which with more modern growing techniques can now supply the European market. They bring new ideas for desserts and can always be mixed into a fruit salad, to which they will add a pleasant flavour, or they can form the basis for a sorbet with a delicate, original taste.

Hints for use
Fresh fruits should always be clean and perfectly fresh.

Damaged fruit can always be used for stewing, even mixed with other fruits.
● Do not hull strawberries until they have been washed.
● Raspberries are so fragile that it is better not to wash them if possible.
● If fruit with stones are to be used in a dessert, always remove the stones.
● For fruits which are to be flambéed or served on a skewer always choose firm fruit.
● In flans or tarts it is possible to add fruit when half cooked or fully cooked, except for fruit with a low water content such as apples.

Nuts

These are also an important ingredient in desserts and their longer period of preservation allows them to be kept in reserve, always ready for use.
● Chestnuts and sweet chestnuts: chestnuts consist of one single round nut, while sweet chestnuts consist usually of two or three smaller, flatter, more triangular nuts joined together. They are in season from the end of September until the end of November.

Choose good nuts which should be heavy, free from marks or holes indicating that the fruit has been attacked by a grub.

Cooked in water in both their skins (the outermost being pierced) or without the outermost skin, chestnuts and sweet chestnuts are peeled after cooking. Used whole for decoration or crushed to a purée, they are used for cakes, sweets or even ice creams.

• Almonds: fresh and dried almonds are available throughout the year. The shells of fresh almonds should be fleshy and free from wrinkles.

Shelled almonds, blanched and toasted are used to decorate cakes but also to make praline (almonds and burnt sugar).

To use almonds, plunge into boiling water to remove the skin more easily (blanching) and thinly slice, crush or chop them.

Chopped and ground almonds, which are commercially produced, are used in many recipes. They do not keep long and should be bought only as you need them.

• Walnuts and hazelnuts: like almonds they can be bought fresh or dried, but there is less difference between the fresh and dried nuts than in the case of almonds. Avoid keeping them too long in a warm place as they will go bad. If kept in a damp place they can take on a mildewy taste. Look out for this mildewy taste in nuts bought ready washed, they may look nicer but their quality is not so good. You can buy shelled walnuts and hazelnuts which do not keep long unless vacuum packed. If you need well-shaped walnut kernels to decorate a cake it is sometimes better to buy them shelled rather than shell them yourself.

Crushed walnuts and hazelnuts can be used as a cake filling or even included in the mixture for some cakes; they can also be used for decoration. Hazelnuts are used to make praline.

• Coconuts: available all year round. The grated white flesh is used mostly in making the mixture for numerous small cakes. If possible, avoid using dried coconut. The milk is pleasant to drink or even to use in cooking. Break with a hammer after draining the milk by perforating the three natural holes in the shell.

Preserved fruit

Fruit can be preserved in several different ways and cannot all be used in the same way.
• Dried or dehydrated fruit: the most common are prunes, raisins, apricots, dates, bananas, pears, apples and even peaches.

They can be eaten alone, stewed, used as part of a fruit salad or as fillings for cakes or charlottes, and of course in recipes which are special to each.

Packets of mixed dried fruits are also widely available.

Raisins must be quickly washed in a colander, dried on kitchen paper and finally steeped in some spirit. Some recipes specify the type of raisin to use, otherwise you can choose whichever you prefer.

Currants are small, black, with a pungent taste.

Sultanas (u.s. seedless white raisins) are golden in colour, larger, sweet and sugary.

California raisins are well-flavoured, seedless and quite large.

Malaga raisins are very big with large pips, often sold in bunches and of remarkable flavour.

Prunes and other dried fruits should have no sign of humidity, but should still be soft, the size being more a matter of price or use than of quality. One can find imported prunes and real Agen prunes, of high quality and popular in France.

• Canned and bottled fruit: prepared in a factory or in the home, sterilised as they are or in syrup, whole or in pieces, they have many uses. They can be added to stewed fruit, used as fillings for flans and tarts or other sweets or added to salads of seasonal fruits.

In syrup: the sugar syrup the fruit is preserved in can also be used in making up a recipe.

In their natural state with sugar added the fruit can be used for any prepared dessert.

You can also preserve your own fruits in jars of different sizes to correspond with their various uses, filling flans and tarts for example.

• Frozen fruit: this method of preservation retains the taste, appearance and nutritive value of the fruit, whether frozen commercially or frozen at home and then kept in the freezer.

The fruits most suitable for freezing are: raspberries, Montmorency cherries, strawberries, bilberries, plums, apricots (halves), apples, etc.

They are used like fresh fruits; for flans and tarts, stewed fruit, fruit salads.

Thawing is a delicate process. If the fruit is to be eaten as fresh fruit it should be thawed slowly (several hours in the bottom of the refrigerator), but it can be quickly thawed, even during cooking, for other uses such as fillings for tarts.

• Fruit preserves: useful in making a certain number of desserts, they play an important part in filling and topping desserts.

Jellies are especially used for icing, for flans or sponge puddings.

Marmalades and jams containing whole fruit or fruit pieces are better for sweets, puddings, charlottes, to fill jam rolls or brioches or pancakes.

• Candied fruit: these fruits are specially prepared and preserved in sugar for decorating cakes. They are widely used often with dried fruit in certain classic recipes: cake, rice pudding, semolina pudding . . .

Angelica comes from the stalk of the angelica plant and is candied in sugar. Other candied fruits include cherries, orange or lemon peel. They keep well in a jar or airtight container.

Flavourings

Flavourings are to a dessert what spices are to cookery – their spirit. They may be liquid, solid or in powder form and their consistency dictates different uses and different methods of mixing into a dish.

Caramel, which is so important in desserts that a section of this book is devoted to it (see page 38), remains the ideal flavouring for a number of creams and sweets.

Liquid flavourings

• Spirits and liqueurs: they are used to flavour cake mixes, sweets, creams, syrups and desserts with a basis of fresh fruit (salads) as well as to moisten babas and savarins and to flambé fruits.

All spirits or liqueurs can be used but it is best to choose those that have the most flavour: rum, brandy, fruit spirits such as plum, pear, kirsch, curaçao, maraschino or aniseed.

In principle, spirits (rum, brandy, fruit spirits) are used in cake making and batters, and fruit brandies and liqueurs are used for creams and sweets.

To moisten babas or savarins use a syrup flavoured with spirits (usually rum), preferably hot.

To add a spirit to a cream or milk-based dish never boil it with the milk, but add it at the end of the process when the cream is warm or even cold.

To flambé a dessert (pudding or fruit for example), warm the spirit in a small saucepan without boiling, sprinkle the dessert with castor sugar, pour over the spirit and flambé. The dessert should be in an ovenproof porcelain or metal dish.

Always avoid desserts flavoured with spirits for young children, replacing this flavouring with a fruit juice for example.

● Orange flower water: often used in the old days to give a pleasant flavour to stewed fruit, creams, fritters and sweet omelettes, orange flower water deserves to be brought back into fashion. It should be used in small quantities as it is very concentrated ($\frac{1}{2}$ to 1 teaspoon).

● Fruit juices: they can be fresh, frozen or canned. You can choose the classic orange or lemon juice or more unusual juices such as pineapple, grapefruit, apricot, cherry, blackcurrant. They can also be mixed to give pleasant, unexpected tastes, either to flavour fruit salads, or to make ice creams or sorbets, or even to flavour sweets: in the latter case do not add them to the milk until the dessert is cold. You can also use fruit juices (particularly orange) to ice certain cakes.

● Liquid essences: some flavourings are found in very concentrated form which should be used in very small quantities, otherwise the taste would be too pronounced: a few drops to 1 teaspoon.

Coffee essence can be bought ready made or made with very strong coffee. You can make it with powdered coffee dissolved at double or triple strength. You will need about 1 tablespoon for 1 litre/$1\frac{3}{4}$ pints of liquid to be flavoured.

Liquid vanilla essence: same proportions.

Pistachio food flavouring: same proportions, a little less if you do not wish the individual flavour to stand out too strongly. Use for ice creams or creams.

Solid flavourings

● Chocolate is one of the most classic dessert flavourings and one of those most enjoyed by children. Not only does it flavour desserts, but as it contains starch it can help to thicken and enrich the dishes to which it is added. Chocolate is used in different forms according to its purpose:

For cake making, use cooking or confectioners' chocolate depending on its purpose. It is usually melted or grated in accordance with the recipe.

Powdered drinking chocolate, which is more practical to use, gives less flavour than block chocolate. You must therefore use more but reduce the quantity of sugar in the recipe. If possible choose cocoa powder which has more flavour, either sweetened or unsweetened. You must take this into account when following the recipe.

Chocolate used to flavour a cream or liquid must be cooked with it.

To use chocolate in a sweet containing no liquid, use block chocolate, melted on a very low heat without adding water or stirring, or cocoa powder if the recipe is sweet enough (mousse, for example).

● Coffee. It is found in different forms and should be chosen in accordance with the recipe.

Coffee beans, which are heated until dry in the oven and then broken into large grains, can be used mixed into a liquid to be flavoured.

Instant coffee powder gives good results. It can be mixed with flour or liquids at any stage of the recipe.

Coffee gives a pleasant flavour to creams, ice creams and sweets. With certain cakes it is also used to flavour both the filling and the icing.

• Vanilla. Like caramel this is one of the great classic dessert flavourings. Vanilla is a dried and treated pod of the vanilla plant and is found in several forms. Do not confuse vanilla, which is a natural product, with vanilline, a manufactured flavouring which is similar in taste.

In its pod form vanilla is placed directly into the liquid to be flavoured and is removed when it has boiled. Cut open the pod lengthways so that the flavour infuses well, for it is the flesh and small seeds which give the flavour.

Vanilla sugar has the double role of flavouring and sweetening simultaneously. It is useful when mixed directly into a mixture containing little or no water, and can be added to the sugar or flour. Take care when buying it that you have not confused it with vanilline sugar. Vanilla sugar may also be prepared at home by placing a vanilla pod in a jar of sugar until the flavour is absorbed. Vanilla is also available in essence form.

If you wish vanilla to keep its flavour it must be stored in an airtight bottle or container.

• Cinnamon. Much used in Anglo-Saxon recipes, cinnamon, which is the inner bark of the cinnamon tree, is becoming better known for its pleasant individual flavour. It is used to flavour stewed and cooked fruit, syrups and some cakes.

Add cinnamon in powder or stick form directly to the liquid before it boils. Use powdered cinnamon in cake mixtures added to the uncooked mixture.

• Peels. Peel is the outer, coloured rind of the skin of a citrus fruit. Lemon, lime and orange peel are normally used.

Avoid the peel of fruit which has been treated. Careful washing is not enough to get rid of the chemicals. Grate or cut into fine strips with a potato peeler, taking only the outside of the skin and avoiding the white part which has a bitter taste. Strips of peel can be used to flavour creams. Remove from the cream when it has boiled.

Peel can be chopped or finely grated and added to cakes, pastry, sweets or fruit salads.

Another method is to rub the skin with cube sugar which will then be used in a recipe. This sugar will give a pleasant flavour to the mixture in which it is used. Peel can be dried in the oven for later use and kept in an airtight container.

• Praline. It is especially used to flavour creams and ice creams. You can buy it ready for use or prepare it yourself: make a light coloured caramel in a pan using 100 g/ 4 oz (U.S. ½ cup) granulated sugar. When ready add 100 g/4 oz (U.S. 1 cup) almonds or hazelnuts, chopped into quite large pieces but not blanched. Cook until the caramel is brown and pour on to a greased marble slab. Leave to cool and break into pieces, then chop or crush with with a rolling pin. Keep in an airtight container and use according to the recipe.

Basic recipes

A rigorous examination of basic recipes and a precise following of their proportions and methods of preparation established by centuries of knowledge and skill handed down from one generation to another will guarantee success.

These recipes, used singly or in combination, are found in many desserts, but often they are not explained in detail. That is why they have been broken down into a number of steps and photographed to show the main stages of their preparation.

With the help of these explanations and illustrations you will be able, with a little care and practice, to launch yourself headlong into dessert making . . . even if up to now you have never turned your hand to pastry making.

Creams

These are the supreme delight, but one may sometimes be afraid to attempt them because their reputation for difficulty used to arise from the imprecise explanations which are usually given. Cooking temperature especially is of supreme importance in the making of creams.

Creams can be flavoured:

With vanilla: 1 pod for each litre/1¾ pints (u.s. 4¼ cups) milk, broken open lengthways and put into the milk before it boils.

With coffee: use 75 g/3 oz coffee beans, lightly crushed and grilled in a pan for each litre/1¾ pints (u.s. 4¼ cups) milk. Add to the boiling milk, infuse for 15 minutes then strain and prepare the cream.

With chocolate: 125 g/4½ oz cooking chocolate for each litre/1¾ pint (u.s. 4¼ cups) milk, melted in the warm milk.

With caramel: (see page 38)

With praline: add 125 g/4½ oz praline (see page 20) to each litre/1¾ pints (u.s. 4¼ cups) cream after it is cooked.

With liqueur: 4 tablespoons (u.s. ⅓ cup) for each litre/1¾ pints (u.s. 4¼ cups) milk, added to the cooled cream.

Custard

A great classic which is pleasantly smooth, but which can separate easily. The adjective 'easy' can be applied to preparing this cream if you know how to do it.

Basic principle: The controlled coagulation of egg yolk in the milk. This always takes place before the temperature reaches 100°C/212°F. It is therefore essential to remove the custard from the heat before it begins to boil. The right moment is when it begins to coat the back of a wooden spoon and the surface froth has disappeared. Stir the custard well in all directions during cooking. This is essential if it is to cook throughout. If you watch it carefully it can be cooked over quite a high heat.

If it goes wrong: if the custard cooks a little too much it will curdle and separate, but all is not lost. Leave to cool, carefully remove the skin and whisk vigorously and it will become smooth again. Do not reheat.

Proportions to serve 6: at least 6 egg yolks, 150 g/5 oz (u.s. ⅔ cup) sugar, 1 litre/1¾ pints (u.s. 4¼ cups) milk, flavouring of your choice: vanilla, caramel, coffee, chocolate, lemon or orange peel, liqueur . . .

Uses

Custard is served cold with brioches and fruit slices.

It is used to pour over puddings and most sweets.

It can be served topped with a dome of whisked egg whites poached in simmering water ('snowy eggs', see page 84), using the whites which are not used for the custard. This custard forms the basis of many ice creams.

1 Place the egg yolks in a basin, sprinkle in the sugar and beat well with a wooden spoon until the mixture becomes frothy.

2 Boil the milk with the pierced vanilla pod (the flavouring most often used).

3 Remove the vanilla pod and pour the boiling milk a little at a time on to the egg and sugar mixture, stirring well, very slowly at first to prevent the eggs curdling. When half the milk has been added you can proceed more quickly.

4 Pour the custard into a heavy-based saucepan. Cook over a low heat, stirring continuously with a wooden spoon, for about 20 minutes. Do not allow to boil.

5 When the froth has completely disappeared and the custard coats the back of a spoon, it is cooked. You must then immediately remove it from the heat.

6 Pour it at once into a cold bowl which helps to cool the custard and to stop it cooking.

Crème pâtissière

This has the reputation of being easier to make than custard and is also thicker since it uses whole eggs and flour. Smooth and melting in the mouth, this is the queen of creams which is eaten alone for the pleasure it gives and which is also found in a number of other desserts.

Basic principles: The rather large amount of flour which it contains thickens when it is cooked, preventing the eggs separating from the liquid when the mixture reaches boiling point. This cream will therefore react better to boiling. It is, however, important to stir it quite vigorously to prevent lumps forming, especially when it begins cooking.

Proportions to serve 6: 2 whole eggs and 4 yolks or 4 whole eggs (the cream will then be thicker), 150 g/5 oz (U.S. $\frac{2}{3}$ cup) sugar, 125 g/4$\frac{1}{2}$ oz (U.S. 1 cup plus 2 tablespoons) flour, 1 litre/1$\frac{3}{4}$ pints (U.S. 4$\frac{1}{4}$ cups) milk, 50 g/ 2 oz (U.S. $\frac{1}{4}$ cup) butter (optional), flavouring: vanilla, caramel, coffee, chocolate . . .

For a lighter cream: it is possible to add to the cooled mixture 2 stiffly whisked egg whites with a little sweetening. This allows you to use the first amount indicated (2 whole eggs and 4 yolks), two of the whites being used in this way.

1 In a basin beat the whole eggs, yolks and sugar until the mixture thickens and becomes pale in colour.

2 Add the sifted flour, then very slowly pour in the boiling milk.

3 Return to the pan and cook over a low heat, stirring continuously with a wooden spoon, until it begins to boil.

4 Remove from the heat (it is definitely unnecessary to cook this cream for longer) and add the butter cut into small lumps together with the flavouring of your choice, except in the case of a vanilla pod which will have already been added to the milk while boiling and then removed.

5 To avoid a skin forming while the cream is cooling, cover the surface with dampened greaseproof paper or sprinkle with castor sugar while still hot.

Uses

Crème pâtissière can be served alone as a sweet, especially flavoured with chocolate or coffee. It is usually served cold, but some people like to eat it whilst still warm.

It is used to fill éclairs, choux pastry, puffs and all sorts of other cakes.

Crème pâtissière is used as the basis of flans, particularly with fruit.

It is the basis of marzipan cream which includes a high proportion of almonds (see page 142).

Cream mould

One of the creams most loved by children, on account of the suspense engendered by its removal from the mould. It is also this cream which is called egg custard, when it is cooked in an ovenproof dish or small individual pots and served in the dish.

Basic principle: Boiling milk is poured on to beaten eggs, with the usual precautions, and then cooked without boiling in a bain marie in the oven or in a bain marie on top of the stove or in a pressure cooker. This cream is normally made in a caramelised mould, except when flavoured with chocolate or coffee.

Choice of mould: You can use a charlotte mould, metal fluted mould (cooking is then easier and quicker), brioche mould or even individual pots.

Proportions to serve 6: 50 g/2 oz cube sugar for the caramel, 500 ml/17 fl oz (u.s. 2 cups) milk, 75 g/3 oz (u.s. 6 tablespoons) castor sugar, 3 whole eggs (or 2 whole plus 2 yolks), 1 vanilla pod or flavourings: coffee, chocolate, fruit juice, orange or lemon rind . . .

1 Prepare the caramel in a saucepan (see page 38), then pour into the mould when it is the required colour, a light mahogany. To cover the mould, hold it with a cloth or oven gloves and tilt in all directions.

2 Boil the milk with the pierced vanilla pod. Add the sugar. When the milk has boiled leave to stand for 5 minutes, then remove the vanilla pod. Whisk the whole eggs vigorously with a fork or electric mixer, then pour in the very hot milk a little at a time, stirring continuously. It is important to pour the milk very slowly at first to prevent the eggs curdling. When about one-third of the liquid is mixed in you can proceed more quickly.

3 Pour the mixture into the caramelised mould. The caramel should be cold. Normally it will have time to cool while you are making the cream. Cook by the chosen method: in a bain marie on top of the stove or in the oven, or in a pressure cooker.

4 Leave to cool in the mould and turn out of the mould when set. It is better to prepare this cream the day before it is required and keep it in the refrigerator overnight.

Cooking methods

In a bain marie on top of the stove: Cooking by this method increases the cooking time and needs a lot of careful attention. It is normally used for individual pots. Take a large shallow saucepan, like a frying pan, or an enamel baking tray; place the pots containing the cream in it, pour hot water into the bottom of the bain marie to the height of the cream. Simmer very gently and remove from the heat immediately the cream has set: you can test it by touching the surface with your fingertip. Care must be taken not to overheat the cream when using this method of cooking.

In a bain marie in the oven: Preheat the oven to moderate (160°C, 325°F, Gas Mark 3). Place the mould containing the cream in an ovenproof dish which is larger than the mould. You can, and it is better to, lift the base of the mould off the container by use of a grill, a folded sheet of paper or a bain marie tray. Pour hot water to the height of the cream and place in the centre of the oven. The bain marie should never boil during cooking, which requires constant watching. The cooking time varies with the size and shape of the mould; individual pots and metal moulds cook more quickly than a large mould. To test if cooked, touch the centre of the cream with the fingertips: it should be slightly resistant to the touch indicating that the sweet is cooked through.

Remove from the oven, leave to cool completely, and chill in the refrigerator.

In a pressure cooker: This is a very quick method of cooking. Pour the hot water into the cooker and place the trivet in the bottom. Stand the filled mould on the trivet, bring to high (15 lb) pressure and cook for 5 minutes. Allow the pressure to reduce at room temperature before removing the lid.

Remove the cream and allow to cool before chilling in the refrigerator.

Removing from the mould: The cream must be perfectly cold. Loosen the edges with the point of a knife. Place the serving dish over the mould, turn over quickly then, when the cream is detached from the mould, remove the mould carefully.

Uses
Moulded cream or egg custard is served alone or with dry sweet biscuits or wafer biscuits. It is also the basis of more elaborate sweets in which it serves to accompany fruit: a crème caramel or crème Chantilly.

Crème Chantilly

Crème Chantilly is a delicious, mouth-watering decoration for many desserts, but it also has a bad reputation for it is considered difficult to thicken. One must know, however, the exact rules to follow in order to succeed.

Basic principles: The cream, bowl and whisk must be cold. Tiny bubbles of air are forced into the cream by whipping; when fully whipped the cream will maintain its shape and may be piped. If whipped too long, the air bubbles will be released, the foam will collapse and yellow butter granules will appear together with watery butter-milk. The difficulty lies therefore in recognising the exact moment when the cream has been whipped sufficiently.

Choosing the cream: Select double or whipping cream which is fresh; when cream is old it becomes thick and acid. Single cream will not whip.

Proportions to serve 4–6: 50 g/2 oz (u.s. ½ cup) icing sugar, 1 (28-g/1-oz) sachet vanilla sugar, 300 ml/½ pint (u.s. 1¼ cups) double cream, 1 or 2 crushed ice cubes.

Keeping the cream: Crème Chantilly can be kept for only a very short time. Really it should be eaten immediately, especially if egg white is added. You can keep it for a few hours in the refrigerator, but no longer. On the other hand it freezes quite well.

Uses
Crème Chantilly is often used to decorate or accompany chilled fruit, ice creams or canned fruits.

It can be used to fill or decorate many cakes: choux pastries, cream sponges, savarins, charlottes, meringues and fruit tarts. It can be flavoured with coffee or chocolate (coffee essence or chocolate powder) and makes a delicious sweet served frozen.

A quick modern method: Whipped cream can be made with evaporated milk in 5 minutes using a (410-g/14½-oz) can unsweetened evaporated milk and 150 g/5 oz (u.s. 1¼ cups) icing sugar which are merely whisked vigorously, adding the chosen flavouring. It froths up well in only a few minutes. This cream can be used in the same way as a crème Chantilly and can be frozen to make a very pleasant ice cream. Leave the can of milk to stand overnight in the refrigerator before using.

1 Add icing sugar and vanilla sugar to the cream with the finely crushed ice cubes. Choose a round-bottomed bowl if using a hand whisk and a tall, narrow container for an electric whisk.

2 Whip the mixture slowly at first, then more and more quickly, checking the thickness of the cream from time to time. When the cream is frothy and forms peaks and the marks of the whisk remain on the surface, stop whipping.

3 To make the cream lighter: fold in a stiffly beaten egg white at the last minute, just before serving.

Cream filling

This is suitable for filling all sorts of cakes; it is very light and very rich. There is no particular obstacle to success if the illustrated recipe is closely followed, but it is essential for a cream of this kind to use only high quality products; butter and eggs must be extra-fresh.

Basic principles: Egg yolks are cooked by the heat of a syrup cooked until it forms threads. This is then added to butter in the same way as a mayonnaise.

Essential precautions: To soften the butter easily it is enough to take it out of the refrigerator an hour or two before use and to rinse the bowl in hot water.

If the eggs are too large the cream may appear to curdle; add a little softened butter and it will return to the right consistency.

This cream easily absorbs smells, so avoid using wooden spoons which have previously been used to make a sauce or for stirring fried onions. When the cream is kept in a refrigerator it must be carefully wrapped.

Proportions to fill and decorate a 25-cm/10-inch cake: 250 g/9 oz cube sugar, 6 tablespoons (u.s. ½ cup) water, 8 egg yolks, pinch of salt, 250 g/9 oz (u.s. 1 cup plus 2 tablespoons) butter, chosen flavouring: 1 teaspoon vanilla or coffee essence, or 2 tablespoons (u.s. 3 tablespoons) unsweetened cocoa powder or praline or liqueur or spirit (rum, kirsch, orange liqueur . . .).

The resulting cream should be very shiny, quite firm yet light and smooth.

Then add the desired flavouring, mixing well.

Keeping the cream: Cream filling can be prepared in advance and kept in the refrigerator either well wrapped or in an airtight container. But do not use it until it has returned to room temperature. Similarly, contrary to general belief, you can keep a cake filled with this cream very well in a refrigerator for several days, providing it is carefully wrapped. It will quickly adapt to room temperature. You are also advised to use this method for some pastries. The cream freezes well.

Uses
The cream is used to fill and decorate many cakes: Genoese, sponge fingers, sponge cakes, mocha, Yule log, charlottes . . . It is not generally eaten alone.

1 Place the sugar and water in a small saucepan. With a hand whisk lightly beat the egg yolks with a pinch of salt.

2 Melt the sugar over a low heat without stirring until completely dissolved, then bring to the boil. The syrup should then be very clear. Boil fiercely for 2 or 3 minutes and check if cooked. Take out a little syrup with a spoon and place in a cold saucer. It should feel sticky to the touch and should crinkle on the surface.

3 Slowly pour the boiling syrup on to the egg yolks, whisking continuously. Leave the mixture until completely cool.

4 Meanwhile cream the butter without melting it. To do so, beat with a wooden spoon or electric mixer until well beaten and smooth. Gradually pour the egg mixture on to the creamed butter, stirring continuously.

Easy butter cream: It can be made quickly with 250 g/ 9 oz (U.S. 1 cup plus 2 tablespoons) butter, 150 g/5 oz (U.S. $\frac{2}{3}$ cup) castor sugar, 2 whole eggs and desired flavouring. This cream is sufficient to fill a 25-cm/10-inch cake.

Break the eggs into a small saucepan and sprinkle on the sugar. Place on a *low* heat and beat with a wooden spoon until the sugar dissolves; there should be no granules left. Leave to cool, stirring frequently. Then cream the butter without melting it, whipping or beating with a wooden spoon after cutting into small pieces. Add the egg and sugar mixture to the butter when quite cold, stirring continuously. The cream should be smooth and firm. Add flavouring.

27

Flan pastries

These are the three queens of desserts: pâte brisée (sweet shortcrust pastry), pâte feuilletée (layered pastry) and pâte sablée (rich flan pastry). They alone are used to make all flans and tarts, and heaven knows how many different sorts there are. But some of these pastries are also used for other sorts of desserts, particularly layered pastry used for turnovers, pies and a host of other small cakes.

It is therefore essential to know how to make them successfully and when you have mastered the method to be able to make them quickly and well, without recourse to a recipe.

Pâte brisée (sweet shortcrust pastry)

The most used, and the most sure of success and currently in favour. You must acquire the technique of a good recipe and stick to it for all dishes – and they are numerous. **Basic principles:** A very quick mixing of the ingredients assures success with this pastry. It should on no account be kneaded and the butter should be 'poorly' mixed in.

Proportions for a 20–25 cm/8–10 inch flan or for 15 small tartlets according to thickness of pastry required: 200 g/7 oz (u.s. 1¾ cups) flour, 100 g/3½ oz (u.s. scant ½ cup) butter, ½ teaspoon salt, 1 tablespoon sugar (optional), about 3 tablespoons (u.s. ¼ cup) water.

1 Place the flour in a bowl and add the butter, cut into very small pieces, with a knife without using the fingers.

2 Make a well, add the salt and sugar and pour in the water a little at a time, mixing quickly with a wooden spoon.

3 Form into a ball with your hands. The pastry should be workable, not sticky and not too soft. Then roll in flour without kneading and leave to stand for 30 minutes if possible. It will then be easier to shape.

4 Shape the pastry with the palm of your hand, crushing the remaining pieces of butter (this is called *fraiser*). This step helps to make the pastry stick together.

5 Fold the pastry into four to make it more crumbly and flaky.

6 Before rolling, very lightly flour the board and rolling pin. Avoid having to re-form into a ball.

7 Do not grease the tin unless the filling contains eggs, sugar and milk. Fold the pastry into four to transfer to the flan ring, then unfold and press it lightly to the sides with the fingertips without tearing it. The pastry can also be lifted over the rolling pin to position it in the flan tin.

8 Trim the pastry by running the rolling pin along the edges of the tin. Pinch with the fingers to form a rim at the edge of the flan. Glaze with egg yolk or sweetened milk.

Cooking: Bake blind in a moderately hot oven (200°C, 400°F, Gas Mark 6) for 15–20 minutes.

The filling is often added after the flan case has been baked blind. To prevent the pastry rising in the centre, prick it with a fork and line with greaseproof paper filled with baking beans.

Keeping: This pastry keeps very well, if wrapped, for a few days in a refrigerator and 3 months in a freezer, but it can dry out and since it is quick to make it is better when possible to make it for immediate use.

Uses
All flans, tarts, turnovers and fruit pastries.

Pâte feuilletée (layered pastry)

We cannot conceal some difficulty in succeeding with this pastry, for it requires time, precision and skill in handling a rolling pin. Nevertheless, with a little care and if you follow the instructions given without trying to take short cuts, you can succeed in making wonderful light pastry.

Basic principles: A certain amount of fat is enclosed in an elastic pastry and by a succession of folds alternate layers of fat and pastry are made which, when cooked, form the flakes of the pastry. That can only succeed if the softened pastry and the fat used have exactly the same consistency. In spite of atmospheric conditions, you must therefore ensure that the butter is neither too soft nor too hard. This is sometimes very difficult to do.

Proportions for a 25-cm/10-inch pie or flan: 200 g/7 oz (u.s. $1\frac{3}{4}$ cups) flour, about 6 tablespoons (u.s. $\frac{1}{2}$ cup) water, the quantity varying with the quality of the flour, $\frac{1}{2}$ teaspoon salt, about 150 g/5 oz (u.s. $\frac{2}{3}$ cup) butter (half the flour and water mixture). The butter can be replaced by margarine.

Cooking: To cook the flan blind, bake in a hot oven (220°C, 425°F, Gas Mark 7) for 15–20 minutes. If it has a filling cook a little more slowly in a moderately hot oven (200°C, 400°F, Gas Mark 6) for 30–35 minutes, covering with foil if becoming too brown.

Keeping the pastry: This type of pastry can be made a little in advance as it keeps well, wrapped in foil, in the bottom of the refrigerator for a day or two. It is best to carry out the last two stages of rolling on the day when it is to be used. It also freezes very well in its uncooked state.

Uses
Pâte feuilletée is used for flans and tarts of all kinds and shapes, also for pies and small cakes such as mille-feuilles.

1 Place the flour in a bowl, make a well, pour in the salted water and gradually mix in, at first with a wooden spoon, then by hand.

2 Work the pastry quickly, form into a ball and weigh it to determine the weight of fat to add to it. Leave to stand for 20 minutes then roll out on a floured board.

3 Cut the butter into small pieces and wrap in the pastry, dampen the edges and join them.

4 Roll the pastry into a long rectangle taking care that no fat escapes, that is by rolling evenly.

5 Fold the obtained rectangle into three, folding one third towards you and one third away from you.

6 Turn the pastry through 90° to the right and carry out the steps for the second time, that is roll again into a rectangle and fold in three in the same way, turn through 90° to the right and leave to stand for 20 minutes in a cool place.

30

7 Take the pastry again, place the opening to the right and in the same way carry out the steps for a third and fourth time, leave to stand then turn again twice more.

8 After these 6 turns the pastry is ready for use. Cutting the pastry will show the layers one above the other. Roll out to a thickness of 8 mm/⅓ inch, pressing evenly on the rolling pin to avoid damaging the flakes. Lift the rolled pastry over a rolling pin on to a pastry board which is merely dampened. It is equally possible to carry out the last stages of preparation directly on the pastry board.

9 With a very sharp knife held vertically, cut a square, rectangle or circle, according to the shape and size of the flan to be made. Remove the left-over pieces from the sides and cut into even strips about 2.5 cm/1 inch wide and the same length as the sides of the pastry.

10 With a little very cold water or even an ice-cube, moisten the edges of the pastry. Lay the strips of pastry along the edges, making sure that they are flat, and press down very lightly with your fingers to ensure that they stick.

11 Prick the whole surface of the flan very evenly with a fork so that it goes right through the pastry. Do not prick the edges.

12 With the point of a knife 'flute' (make slight cuts) along the inside and outside edges of the pastry so that the edges will rise better during cooking.

The pastry should then be cooked blind without its filling and can be filled afterwards with uncooked fruit and jam – strawberries and redcurrant jelly, for example – or crème pâtissière and cooked fruit, apricots, pears, plums . . .

31

13 The pastry can also be cooked with a filling of non-juicy fruit such as apples. Arrange slices of apple (preferably cooking apples) on the base of the flan.

14 Glaze the edges of the pastry with beaten egg, taking care not to leave any drips which could prevent the flakes separating when they rise, sprinkle with sugar and add a few small pieces of butter.

Pâte sablée (rich flan pastry)

This is a fine, short pastry which crumbles in the mouth, from which fact doubtless its name arises. It is used both for sweet biscuits and for sophisticated tarts and flan cases.

Basic principles: The very crumbly nature of this pastry is obtained by the way in which the various ingredients are mixed and kneaded.

It is important to stick rigidly to the amount of flour and to add it all at once. Then you must on no account add more or the proportions will be spoiled.

Proportions for a 20–25 cm/8–10 inch flan or about 15 small tartlets, or 20 small open tarts: 125 g/4½ oz (U.S. generous ½ cup) sugar, 1 egg, ¼ teaspoon salt, 250 g/9 oz (U.S. 2¼ cups) flour, 125 g/4½ oz (U.S. generous ½ cup) butter, flavouring: lemon peel, vanilla or rum (optional).

Cooking: Pâte sablée is cooked in a moderately hot oven (200°C, 400°F, Gas Mark 6) for 15–20 minutes. When cooked, it should be a pale golden colour. As soon as it is cooked, loosen the pastry from the baking sheet or flan tin and cool on a cooling tray.

Leave large tarts or flans to cool before removing from the tin, for when hot this pastry is quite crumbly and breaks easily.

Keeping: Small sweet biscuits made with pâte sablée pastry will easily keep for 2 weeks in an airtight container.

Uses
Numerous tarts and flan cases. All sorts of sweet biscuits which can be made in many pleasing shapes.

1 Place the sugar in a bowl and add the egg and salt.

2 Beat the mixture with a wooden spoon until creamy: it should double in volume.

3 Add the sifted flour all at once. To begin with, mix with a wooden spoon.

4 Lift the mixture with the fingers: it should not stick together, but separate into small grains. This operation is called 'sanding' the pastry.

5 When it forms small grains, tip it on to the pastry-board and place the butter in the centre.

6 Knead the butter into the grains with the hands. If well kneaded it will not stick to the fingers. Form into a ball, scrape the board and flour lightly.

7 Roll out the pastry. To line a large tin transfer the pastry over the rolling pin. To make small tarts cut pieces of pastry to the shape of the tart tins but a little larger, and press into these tins without stretching the pastry. Prick the pastry with a fork if cooking blind.

Other basics

Pancake batter, choux pastry and yeast dough must be added to the three pastries already given to complete the range of basic recipes for the desserts.

Pancake batter

Pancake batters differ according to whether they are based on beer, milk, water or egg whites.

A mixture of half water, half milk gives excellent results. By increasing the amount of melted butter, the flavour is finer and the batter needs less fat for cooking.

Below is the recipe for a classic batter.

Basic principle: It is a simple mixture of all the ingredients, to give a very uniform batter, perfectly fluid and spreading well in the frying pan during cooking.

Proportions for 15–18 medium-sized quite thin pancakes: 250 g/9 oz (U.S. 2¼ cups) flour, 25 g/1 oz (U.S. 2 tablespoons) castor sugar, ½ teaspoon salt, 50 g/2 oz (U.S. ¼ cup) melted butter or 2 tablespoons (U.S. 3 tablespoons) oil, 500 ml/17 fl oz (U.S. 2 cups) milk (or half water, half milk), 3 eggs, flavouring: vanilla or rum (1 teaspoon) or grated lemon peel.

1 Place the flour in a bowl, make a well and in the centre place the sugar, salt and melted butter or oil. Add about half the liquid.

2 Mix in beginning at the centre; when all the flour is mixed in the batter should be scarcely fluid. To make it perfectly smooth beat vigorously with a wooden spoon.

3 Add the beaten eggs then add the rest of the liquid. The batter should be smooth and fluid but not over-fluid. Add the flavouring and leave to stand for 1 hour (optional).

4 Grease the frying pan using a cloth tied over a fork or wooden spoon and heat the pan.

5 Into the hot pan pour half a ladle of batter and tilt the pan in all directions very quickly to shape the first pancake.

6 Turn the pancake with a palette knife or spatula as soon as it becomes free from the pan, or if you are good at it, toss it. Sugar or fill the pancakes as they are cooked, and if not eaten immediately, keep hot.

34

To keep hot

In a bain marie: As the pancakes are cooked, pile them on to a plate placed over a saucepan two-thirds full of simmering water. Cover with foil or another plate.

In the oven: Unfilled pancakes can be wrapped in foil and left in a cool oven (140°C, 275°F, Gas Mark 1) for 10–15 minutes. If they are filled, the filling will prevent them drying out and it is sufficient then to arrange them on a plate and to reheat them in a cool oven for a few minutes without covering.

Keeping pancakes: You can prepare pancakes in advance and keep them in the refrigerator for 24 hours in a sheet of foil; reheat them in the oven or in a frying pan with a knob of butter. They also freeze well.

Choux pastry

It is used for making many pastries, both large and small, and has the advantage of cooking without moulds. It is economical for it goes a long way.

Basic principles: Contrary to other methods used in pastry making choux pastry is cooked twice, first on top of the stove as it is prepared and a second time in the oven on a baking sheet, or it can be fried.

The flour, which is added all at once to a boiling mixture of water and fat, swells and forms a paste. The thickness of this paste depends on the proportion of water to flour and on the size of the eggs. Sometimes, if they are very large, do not add all the last egg.

Proportions to make about 20 choux (allowing 1 scant tablespoon mixture for each) or 30 small choux (allowing 1 teaspoon mixture for each): 75 g/ 3 oz (U.S. 6 tablespoons butter), 250 ml/8 fl oz (U.S. 1 cup) water, ½ teaspoon salt, 1 tablespoon sugar, 150 g/5 oz (U.S. 1¼ cups) flour, 4 eggs.

1 Cut the butter into small pieces and place in a saucepan with the water, salt and sugar. Bring to the boil, heating the mixture slowly so that the butter is completely melted by the time the mixture boils.

2 When boiling, remove the pan from the heat, add all the sifted flour at once and stir briskly with a wooden spoon.

3 The dough should form a ball which comes away from the sides of the pan. Replace over a low heat for a few seconds, stirring to dry it out.

4 Remove from the heat, beat in the first egg then the others one at a time; the mixture will then become less solid. Mix very carefully.

5 The resulting dough should resemble a stiff paste. It is now ready to be cooked in the oven.

6 Grease a baking sheet then place the choux pastry on it, either in spoonfuls or piped using a large piping tube. It is possible to make choux into a variety of different shapes and sizes.

Cooking: The baking of the choux varies according to the way in which they are to be used. Cook in a hot oven (220°C, 425°F, Gas Mark 7) for 15–20 minutes for very light, airy choux which must be eaten the same day. Cooked in a moderately hot oven (200°C, 400°F, Gas Mark 6) for 30–40 minutes, the choux buns will be drier and more solid. They will keep better and will be able to be used for making into larger cakes. A well-cooked choux should be very light and a little firm.

Uses
Round or oval choux of all sizes, éclairs, religieuses, Paris-Brest cakes, Saint-Honoré, small choux buns, profiteroles . . .

Icing choux pastry

In a saucepan prepare a caramel of a light golden colour with 100 g/4 oz cube sugar, just enough water to moisten the sugar and ½ teaspoon vinegar.

Holding the choux bun by the base, quickly dip the top into the caramel and leave to cool. (Take care or you can get a very painful burn.)

This amount of caramel is enough to ice about 15 choux buns at one time, but no more as the caramel becomes too dark.

Yeast dough (baba dough)

We are here describing dough made with baker's yeast which is organic in origin, not a dough using a chemical yeast, for their uses and the results they produce are very different. It is a delicious dough which when soaked in a liquid gives light cakes of the type that one 'can eat without being hungry'.

Basic principles: It is the same as bread dough. The yeast, made up of microscopic fungi, ferments the sugar and flour. During the rising of the dough the carbon dioxide gas forms bubbles which are released causing the dough to rise which gives the baked bread its characteristic structure.

Humidity and a warm atmosphere are conditions essential for fermentation to take place.

The ingredients used for the baba should preferably be left to stand in the room so that all are at the same temperature: the eggs should be taken out of the refrigerator in advance, the butter should be melted and cooled, the bowl should be warmed by rinsing in hot water and then dried.

Proportions to serve 6: 150 g/5 oz (U.S. 1¼ cups) flour, 1 teaspoon sugar, ½ teaspoon salt, 2 eggs, 15 g/½ oz fresh yeast, 3 tablespoons (U.S. ¼ cup) milk, 75 g/3 oz very soft butter.

The baba should steep in the rum syrup for at least 2 hours before serving, filled with fruit, cream or as it is.

1 Sift the flour into a basin and make a well in the centre. Place in it the sugar, salt and the two beaten eggs.

2 Crumble the yeast into warm milk: the temperature should be between 30°C/86°F and 35°C/95°F; any hotter it will kill the living cells in the yeast.

3 Add the yeast liquid to the centre of the well, stir gently beginning at the centre, add the butter and stir.

4 When the dough is well mixed, cover the bowl with a lightly floured tea towel and leave to stand in a warm, draught-free place for 2–3 hours. The exact length of time for the rising of the dough depends on the surrounding temperature.

5 When the dough has finished rising, it should have doubled in size. Using your hand, knock back the dough without beating. The dough should fall again.

6 Generously grease the tin, fill one third full (never more) and leave to stand a little longer (the dough should reach 1 cm/½ inch from the top edge of the tin). Then bake in a hot oven (220°C, 425°F, Gas Mark 7) for 25–30 minutes.

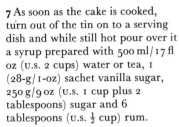

7 As soon as the cake is cooked, turn out of the tin on to a serving dish and while still hot pour over it a syrup prepared with 500 ml/17 fl oz (U.S. 2 cups) water or tea, 1 (28-g/1-oz) sachet vanilla sugar, 250 g/9 oz (U.S. 1 cup plus 2 tablespoons) sugar and 6 tablespoons (U.S. ½ cup) rum.

Cooking: The baba is cooked in a hot oven (220°C, 425°F, Gas Mark 7) for 25–30 minutes until golden brown. It should not rise any more in the oven.

Uses
Baba dough can be made into cakes of various shapes, large or individual crowns made in dariole moulds for example. The pastry can be enriched by adding raisins or candied fruit. It may be decorated in several ways: strawberries, oranges, pineapple, fruit salad, preserved fruit, crème Chantilly, crème pâtissière or even ice cream.

Caramel

Easy to make and economical, which in itself is important, caramel can be either a flavouring or a decoration, or both together, and it gives desserts an old-world atmosphere which is as reassuring as a childhood memory. Once again you must know how to make it practically, whatever the use for which the caramel is intended.
Basic principles: Caramel is one of the stages in the cooking of sugar, obtained quite simply by heating then boiling sugar and water. When it has reached a certain stage of cooking the sugar becomes a beautiful golden colour.

Never make the caramel directly in a mould but in a small saucepan with a heavy base (untinned copper, aluminium or stainless steel).
Proportions: 100 g/4 oz cube sugar, 3–4 tablespoons (U.S. ¼–⅓ cup) water, a little vinegar or lemon juice so that the caramel stays liquid longer. This amount is enough to caramelise a medium-sized mould.

You also need 3 tablespoons (U.S. ¼ cup) warm water to dilute the caramel if used to flavour milk.

To decorate choux pastry with caramel, add vinegar or lemon juice to the caramel. Prepare the caramel in a small pan and dip the choux buns into it one at a time holding them by the base. Leave to cool (see page 36).

Colour of the caramel

Very pale: stop cooking as soon as the edges of the pan begin to colour. This almost white caramel is used for icing petits fours and caramelised fruit.
Light or golden: to coat cream-filled choux buns and buns which are to be arranged as a set piece.
Medium: most often used to caramelise moulds and to flavour puddings, creams, rice cakes, etc.
Brown: the flavour becomes very bitter. If a caramel has accidentally become chestnut coloured, do not use it.

1 Place the sugar cubes in a saucepan and dampen them with water. Place the pan on a gentle heat.

2 When the sugar has dissolved, bring to the boil. You must watch it carefully during cooking.

3 Shake the pan from time to time so that it cooks evenly, but it is important that you do not use a spatula, spoon or fork to stir the sugar. When the caramel is the required colour remove the pan from the heat.

4 To caramelise a mould, pour all the hot caramel into the base of the mould, hold in both hands using a tea towel or oven gloves and tip in all directions so that the caramel is well spread. Leave to cool.

5 To flavour milk with caramel, pour 3 tablespoons (u.s. ¼ cup) warm water into the boiling caramel. This is called quenching it.

6 Replace the caramel over a low heat stirring a little, then pour into the hot milk.

Equipment, cooking and finishing touches

How should you cook a cake? In what kind of tin? Often recipes say nothing or very little on this subject. It is, however, essential to know in many cases. And then there is the presentation of the dessert which is so important if it is to please the eye as well as the palate. Filling and icing cakes – does this only concern a professional pastry cook or should you try your hand? The following pages are intended to reassure the least expert of cooks, to give them the courage to try and . . . the secret of success.

Equipment

The tin makes the cake . . .

Yes, it is the tin that makes the cake for it gives it its shape and size. But that is not all: it guarantees success as long as it is wisely chosen.

In fact, if the old-fashioned charm of shaped moulds is appealing, it must be remembered that they are the fruit of years of experience which have led to the perfecting of these shapes, each one becoming traditionally linked to a particular cake.

Just as you would not make a stew in a frying pan or a tart in a kugelhopf mould, so you need a round ring tin for a savarin and a fluted mould for a brioche.

Tart or flan tins: useful to have a few of different sizes. Avoid choosing too light a metal. Choose them of galvanized steel, quite thick, with fixed or loose base, the latter being useful for turning out flans which have stuck. Certain modern non-stick tins also allow easy turning out. Fluted edges will make more attractive flans. Nowadays you can find old-fashioned flan dishes in ovenproof porcelain which are suitable for some fragile flans as they allow them to be served from the dish. Dishes in ovenproof glass give equally good results. Cooking time will be a little longer for the dish takes longer to warm up than a metal one.

There are also flan rings which allow flans to be made directly on a baking sheet, and last of all small, individual tartlet tins, round or in the shape of little boats which are fun to use, if only to use up left-over pastry.

Current sizes: 15–25 cm/6–10 inches in diameter. We recommend a 18-cm/7-inch tin to serve 4, 25-cm/10-inch to serve 6.

Loaf tins: rectangular, with smooth base and sides. A loaf tin in galvanised steel will not rust. Tins are available which can be taken apart but there is a chance that the mixture may run out at the joints. Usual sizes are 0.5 kg/ 1 lb and 1 kg/2 lb, the smaller being the most useful size. It is best to have two tins as it is as easy to make two cakes as one and they can be cooked together. In addition, cake keeps well (several weeks if necessary). When baking a cake, cooking will be much more even if the tin is lined with greased greaseproof paper, as the paper acts as an insulator.

Cake tins: round, square or oblong. Normally they are smooth-sided but can be fluted. They range in size from 15–30 cm/6–12 inches in diameter. A round cake tin gives the best baking results, the edges being equidistant from the centre. It is also best to choose a tin made in galvanized steel which is traditional. Other materials (ovenproof porcelain, which avoids the need to turn the dessert out of the tin to serve; non-stick aluminium which on the contrary makes turning out easy) can also be chosen for some recipes.

Savarin, baba and crown moulds: they have a large boss in the centre. They are also used for rice and semolina cakes, sweets and flans, puddings and some moulded creams, for which they are advantageous in two ways: a pleasant presentation allowing a filling of fruit, cream, etc. in the centre, and ease of cooking, for the dough or cream will not be very thick and thus will cook or set more evenly and more quickly. They are to be found in galvanized steel or non-stick aluminium and in several sizes.

flan tins

cake tin

baba mould

savarin mould

loaf tin

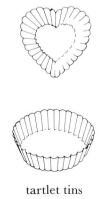

tartlet tins

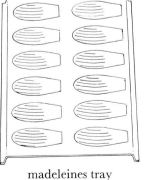

madeleines tray

41

charlotte mould

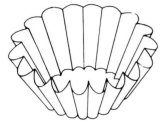

brioche mould

Charlotte mould: a deep smooth-sided mould, with slightly sloping sides, and sometimes a lid. Usually 10–18 cm/4–7 inches in diameter.

The charlotte mould should be lined with greaseproof paper if using acid fruit to avoid oxydisation.

Brioche mould: its base is flat but its edges are widely fluted and widely sloping. Diameters range from 6–25 cm/2½–10 inches. This mould is used for brioches, but also for puddings and rice and semolina cakes. You can buy brioche moulds in tin, galvanized steel, in oven-proof glass and non-stick aluminium. Same remarks apply as for the other moulds.

Kugelhopf mould: these moulds used to be made of glazed earthenware which allowed the dough to rise very well. The mould has a central boss and slanting fluted sides; almonds are placed at the base of each flute. Sizes vary from 19–24 cm/7½–9½ inches in diameter, the exterior diameter being clearly larger than the diameter at the base. Kugelhopf moulds can also be used to give an attractive shape to flans and moulded creams.

Other moulds: there are a host of other more specialised tins – bun tins, petits fours tins, small rounded moulds, Bavarian cake moulds.

Everyone must choose which to use according to the end product.

Caring for your moulds
Always wash moulds carefully and dry them well. Avoid scratching them with scouring pads. If the cake has stuck to the tin, soak in hot water; the same applies to caramel. If your tins are to have a long life never prepare a caramel in them directly, but cook in a small saucepan and pour into the tin.

terrine

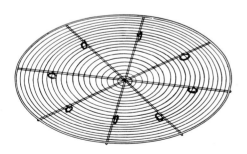

wire cooling tray

whisks

ice cream scoop

Never cut a cake in the tin; the point of the knife will leave scratch marks which will make the next cake stick. To keep tin moulds free from rust, grease them lightly and wrap in paper.

Lining a tin
Use greaseproof paper; it should cover the inside of the tin exactly and the edges of the paper should overlap slightly. You can also line a tin with foil.

Basic equipment
Good baking tins are essential but you must also have other well-chosen items:
• Bowls or dishes in glazed earthenware or in ovenproof glass in which you can prepare mixtures.
• Spatulas and wooden spoons. Avoid using them for other cooking which can give them a taste incompatible with dessert making.
• A hand whisk used to beat many mixtures. It is useful even if you have a mechanical or electric whisk.
• A pastry brush to glaze pastries and grease tins.
• A pastry board or smooth surface which can be kept perfectly clean for rolling out pastry.
• A rolling pin; choose a simple one in a hard wood, beech or boxwood.
• Pastry cutters to cut the pastry into various shapes and a wheel to cut pastry. These are small accessories which are not essential, but which save time and give a pleasant effect.
• Kitchen scales are essential since in cake making nothing can be made without weighing. A graduated measuring jug is also useful for liquids.
• A cooling tray.
• A palette knife to loosen cakes from the tin, and for icing cakes.
• A piping bag and nozzles to give an attractive finish to a dessert.
• An ice cream scoop; makes handling ice cream a lot easier and gives a professional touch.

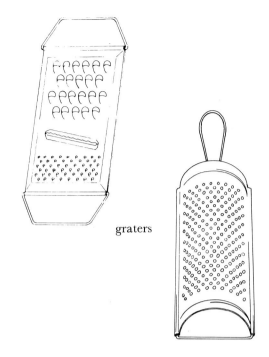

graters

spatula

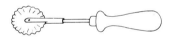

pastry wheel

nutcrackers

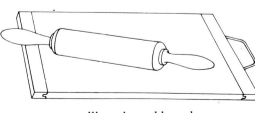

rolling pin and board

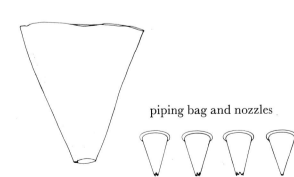

piping bag and nozzles

43

Baking cakes

Colour, flavour and rising are very important in cake making, but baking is made easy today by the precision of oven temperatures. Cakes brown and become firm at a steady temperature which is easily controlled.

The thermostat is essential for cooking successfully. Set it to the number indicated in the recipe (see table).
● Place the shelf at the correct height before lighting the oven.
● Preheat the oven.
● When regulating the oven take the following into account:
　– the composition of the mixture: cakes containing a lot of sugar or eggs generally bake in quite a cool oven.
　– the size of the cakes: small or shallow cakes cook faster than large, deep ones. For large cakes, lower the temperature and increase the cooking time.
　– for a soft cake such as a whisked sponge you need quite a hot oven; for a crisper cake such as a Victoria sandwich or shortbread, a cooler oven, as cooking dries out the mixture.

If cakes which are cooked for a long time, e.g. very rich fruit cakes, become too brown, cover the top with a sheet of foil or folded newspaper.

The best place for a cake is usually the middle of the oven, but if you want the top to caramelise, you must place it near the top of the oven and eventually finish cooking under the grill. Never open the oven door during the initial stage of cooking.

A cake made with dried yeast or beaten egg whites should be cooked in a moderate oven, so that the cake has time to rise before becoming completely solid. Cakes made with fresh yeast need quite a hot oven to kill the yeast and prevent the mixture rising any more as it has already fully risen before it is put in the oven.

A cake is cooked when:
● a dry knife, trussing needle or steel skewer comes out of it clean. If the mixture sticks to it, the cake is not completely cooked.
● it reaches the right colour, unless it has been cooked too quickly and the top of the cake has burnt slightly.

44

Table for baking cakes and pastries

Oven temperature	Degrees Celsius	Degrees Fahrenheit	Gas Mark		Average time	Remarks
Very cool	110	225	$\frac{1}{4}$	meringues (individual)	3–4 hours	
Cool	140	275	1	reheating some desserts (such as small pies, pancakes)	about 10–20 minutes	depending on size. Cover with foil to prevent drying out
				very rich fruit cakes	4 hours	for a 20-cm/8-inch cake
Moderate	160	325	3	ring or finger biscuits	20 minutes	should brown at the edges for a 20–cm/8-inch cake
				Victoria sandwich (creamed cake)	35–40 minutes	
				Madeira cake (creamed cake)	$1\frac{1}{2}$–$1\frac{3}{4}$ hours	for a 18-cm/7-inch cake
				semi-rich fruit cakes	$1\frac{1}{2}$–2 hours	for a 18-cm/7-inch cake
				cream moulds (e.g. crème caramel)	about 1 hour	place in the centre of the oven
Moderate	180	350	4	whisked sponge cakes	30–35 minutes	for a 20-cm/8-inch cake
				macaroons	15–20 minutes	place in the top or centre of the oven
Moderately hot	200	400	6	pâte sablée	15 minutes	made into biscuits
				pâte brisée (cooked blind)	15–20 minutes	
				choux pastry	20–30 minutes	place near the top of the oven
				fruit flans (filled)	45 minutes	
				(cooked blind)	15–20 minutes	place near the top of the oven
				Swiss roll (whisked sponge)	10–12 minutes	place near the top of the oven
				Kugelhopfs	about 1 hour	reduce temperature to 190°C, 375°F, Gas Mark 5 after 20 minutes
Hot	220	425	7	pâte feuilletée (filled)	30–35 minutes	
				(cooked blind)	15–20 minutes	
				babas (yeast dough)	25–30 minutes	cook in a 20-cm/8-inch mould
Hot	230	450	8	small brioches	10 minutes	
				small puff pastries (palm leaves, pastry sticks)	about 8–10 minutes	
				browning meringue (e.g. Norwegian omelettes)	2–3 minutes	just time to lightly brown and set the meringue

45

Measuring without kitchen scales (level spoons and cups)

Ingredient	Measure (level)	Weight in grams/ounces		Ingredient	Measure (level)	Volume in ml/fl oz
castor sugar	teaspoon	5 g		oil	teaspoon	5 ml
	tablespoon	15 g			tablespoon	15 ml
	cup	200 g/7 oz			cup	210 ml/7 fl oz
cube sugar	small	2 g		water	teaspoon	5 ml
	average	4 g			tablespoon	15 ml
butter	½ teaspoon or knob	3 g			cup	210 ml/7 fl oz
	teaspoon or large knob	7 g		milk	tablespoon	20 ml
	tablespoon	18 g/½ oz			cup	220 ml/7½ fl oz
flour	teaspoon	4 g				
	tablespoon	12 g				
	cup	100–110 g/4 oz				
tapioca	tablespoon	12 g				
cornflour	tablespoon	12 g				
salt	teaspoon	8 g				
	tablespoon	25 g				
instant coffee	teaspoon	2 g				
	tablespoon	6 g				
semolina	tablespoon	15 g				
rice	tablespoon	15 g				

All conversions are approximate. The weights have been rounded off to the nearest useful measure for the purposes of the recipes. Weights and measures of specific ingredients may vary with altitude, humidity, variation in method of preparation, etc.

The final stages

Before cooking

Glazing is intended to give pastry tarts or flans, pies and small tarts a beautiful golden colour and a shine which makes them appetising as soon as they come out of the oven. Glaze the pastry with a soft brush just before putting it into the oven. Use an egg yolk diluted in a little milk or water (you can keep back a little yolk for this purpose if eggs have been used in the recipe), a mixture of milk and sugar, a little egg white or if you have nothing better, a little water or milk which will make the pastry shine.

• Castor sugar will make tarts, sweets and palmleaf pastries shine if sprinkled on just before cooking so that it caramelises during cooking.

• Caramel gives cakes and puddings or moulded creams a beautiful amber-coloured appearance if you take the trouble to coat the tin with it (see caramel, page 38).

Just before the end of cooking

• Italian meringue is used to decorate some desserts: filled sponge cakes, Norwegian omelettes, fruit tarts . . . Stiffly whisk the egg whites (1 white to 50 g/2 oz (u.s. ¼ cup) sugar). Dissolve the sugar slowly and cook until it forms a ball, that is when a small amount dropped in cold water can be rolled into a ball between the fingers. Pour the boiling sugar syrup slowly down the edge of the bowl containing the whisked egg whites and beat vigorously: the mixture should rise and become very shiny.

Cover the top and sides of the dessert and place in a hot oven (230°C, 450°F, Gas Mark 8) for a few minutes to brown the surface.

• Caramelised sugar: generously sprinkle fruit tarts or sponges with granulated, castor or, better still, icing sugar just before they finish cooking. Return to the hot oven for a few minutes to caramelise.

After cooking

The filling

Cakes which are dry in texture are usually filled to make them softer and give more flavour: for example, slices, sponge fingers, sponge cakes, brioches, rolls and logs. Cut the cake horizontally into two or three with a very sharp or electric knife, keeping the cake flat to avoid breaking it. Lightly moisten the cake with liqueur diluted in water, with a very light jam sauce or with fruit juice. Spread the chosen filling over each piece then sandwich the cake together. The cake can also be covered with the filling, using a palette knife, or iced.

Icing

Contrary to general belief, it is not difficult to ice successfully. It is important always to use icing sugar and to

choose the flavour to match the cake: orange juice for an orange cake, coffee or chocolate for éclairs and choux pastries or the same liqueur that flavours the cake or the cream served with it.

If you add candied fruit or coffee beans or other additional decoration, these must be placed on the cake immediately after icing before it dries to avoid cracking the icing if done later. Cakes are usually iced cold.

Glacé icing:

With water

200 g/7 oz (u.s. 1½ cups) icing sugar, about 2–3 tablespoons (u.s. 3–4 tablespoons) water. Gradually stir the water into the sugar and beat well. When the consistency is thick and no longer runs, spread with a palette knife or wide-bladed knife. Smooth the icing and allow to cool or dry out at room temperature.

With fruit juice

Made in the same way but replacing the water with orange or lemon juice.

With liqueur

1–2 tablespoons (u.s. 2–3 tablespoons) liqueur to 100 g/ 4 oz (u.s. scant cup) icing sugar; the liqueur can be warmed in a bain marie.

With coffee

Replace the water with very strong coffee made either with instant coffee dissolved in a little water or coffee essence added to a few drops of water if necessary.

White royal icing

225 g/8 oz (u.s. 1¾ cups) icing sugar, 1 egg white, few drops lemon juice. Mix the ingredients together and beat until the icing is smooth and shiny. Quickly spread over the cake with a palette knife.

Chocolate icing

In a small basin over a saucepan of hot water melt 125 g/ 4½ oz plain chocolate. When smooth add 6 tablespoons (u.s. ½ cup) double cream and continue stirring. Pour this warm icing over the cake and spread with a palette knife. The icing will keep its shine when it dries.

Fondant icing

Fondant icing is a white, smooth mixture made with sugar, water and glucose which is cooked until the soft ball stage is reached, 116°C/240°F, or when the mixture forms a ball between the fingers.

It is then poured on to a marble slab and worked until smooth and white. Fondant icing can be left white, coloured or flavoured and can be bought ready made. It is used for petits fours, sugared fruit, choux pastries and all kinds of cakes.

Warm the fondant in a basin over a saucepan of hot water and stir with a wooden spoon. Add the flavouring – spirits, coffee essence, cocoa powder – but be careful of liquid flavourings which can make the icing too runny. Fondant should have a coating consistency. Do not heat beyond 35–40°C/95–104°F, or it will lose its shine. Brush the cake with sieved apricot jam and pour the fondant over the cake, tilting in all directions to make it run and cover the sides. Smooth with a knife, dipping the blade into hot water. Leave to cool.

Decoration

Caramel

This is used to decorate many cakes after cooking (see page 38).

Almond paste

You can buy it ready made like fondant icing, but you can also make it yourself. Mix 100 g/4 oz (u.s. scant cup) icing sugar with 1 teaspoon rice flour, 1 tablespoon kirsch and 1 or 2 tablespoons (u.s. 2 or 3 tablespoons) water to give a thick paste. Gradually add 100 g/4 oz (u.s. 1 cup) ground almonds. When the mixture becomes too thick to mix with a wooden spoon, knead it by hand. Roll out the almond paste on a board sprinkled with icing sugar. Cover the whole cake with this paste or use small pieces of it to make amusing decorations for special occasion cakes. The shapes can be cut out with a knife or modelled with the fingers.

Sauces

They are quicker to make than creams and can be used to coat a dessert, to pour over a cake, or to serve with ice cream or rice pudding.

Jam sauce: Bring to the boil 3 tablespoons (u.s. $\frac{1}{4}$ cup) jam (apricot, orange, blackcurrant, etc), juice of $\frac{1}{2}$ lemon and a few spoonfuls of water in a small saucepan. If preferred, jam sauce may be sieved before using.

Chocolate sauce: Place in a basin over hot water, 125 g/ $4\frac{1}{2}$ oz chocolate, broken into pieces, and a large knob of butter. Stir well and add 2 or 3 tablespoons (u.s. 3 or 4 tablespoons) water when the chocolate is fully melted. Pour over ice cream or fruit. Serve at once.

Caramel sauce: Into a prepared caramel pour a little milk, double cream or evaporated milk and serve with ice cream, puddings or egg custards.

Other decorations

● Icing sugar sprinkled through a fine sieve on to a cake covered with chocolate icing forms a simple decoration. Or place a doily on top of the cake and sprinkle with sieved icing sugar. Remove the doily taking care not to disturb the design.
● Walnuts and hazelnuts, crushed or chopped toasted almonds, crushed praline sprinkled on the top of a cake.
● Fresh, candied or canned fruit placed on a cake or on ice cream.
● Powdered or grated chocolate, chocolate caraque (made with a potato peeler), or chocolate vermicelli bought ready-made.
● Candied coffee beans, Toulouse violets or sugared almonds on a christening cake.

All forms of decoration are possible by mixing techniques and flavours to create cakes for any occasion which can be amusing, sometimes sumptuous and always delicious.

Some ideas for filling and decorating bought cakes or cakes made in advance

Soak with	Fill with	Icing	Decoration
sweetened water and liqueur	canned fruit, drained (e.g. pineapple) plus jam (e.g. apricot)	sieved jam	candied fruit
sweetened water and rum	chocolate mousse or crème Chantilly	chocolate fondant	whole nuts
sweetened water and rum	mocha cream	mocha cream and toasted, sliced almonds	almonds or Toulouse violets
strong black coffee	chocolate cream	coffee icing	candied coffee beans or chocolate caraque
sweetened water and kirsch	fresh strawberries or raspberries and crème Chantilly or cream cheese	sieved icing sugar	fresh strawberries or raspberries
sweetened water and rum	chestnut cream and whipped cream	melted chocolate	glacé chestnuts
sweetened water and calvados	stewed apple and crème pâtissière	glacé icing flavoured with calvados	candied angelica
sweetened water and kirsch	raspberry jam	Italian meringue	fresh raspberries
sweetened water and kirsch	blackcurrant jelly and ground almonds	glacé icing flavoured with kirsch	
sweetened water and maraschino	crème pâtissière and steeped candied fruit	Italian meringue	candied fruit

One Hundred Desserts

Apple charlotte

Preparation time: 30 minutes
Cooking time: 40 minutes
Oven temperature: moderately hot (200°C, 400°F, Gas Mark 6)

METRIC/IMPERIAL
1 kg/2 lb cooking apples
3 tablespoons water
about 100 g/4 oz sugar
575–675 g/1¼–1½ lb stale crustless
   bread
about 100 g/4 oz butter
Custard: illustrated recipe, page 22

AMERICAN
2 lb baking apples
¼ cup water
about ½ cup sugar
1¼–1½ lb stale crustless bread

about ½ cup butter
Custard: illustrated recipe, page 22

Peel, core and thickly slice the apples. Place in a large saucepan with the water. Cover and cook over a moderate heat for about 10 minutes until soft. Remove from the heat and beat with a wooden spoon, adding the sugar.

Generously grease an 18-cm/7-inch charlotte mould. Slice the bread and remove any crusts, then butter the slices. Cut about one-third into triangles and the rest into rectangles.

Line the base of the mould with half of the bread triangles, buttered sides uppermost, overlapping slightly.

Then cover the sides of the mould with buttered rectangles. Overlap them with the buttered sides innermost in the same way.

Pour the stewed apple into the centre and cover with the remaining triangles of bread. Bake in a moderately hot oven for 40 minutes. The bread should be well browned.

Remove from the oven but do not remove from the mould until the last moment.

The charlotte can be served hot, warm or cold according to taste. Serve by itself or with a vanilla custard (see page 22).

Serves 6

Normandy pancakes

Preparation time: 10 minutes for the batter; 20 minutes for the filling
Standing time for the batter: 2 hours if possible
Cooking time: 10 minutes for the apples; 3 minutes each for the
  pancakes; 5 minutes in the oven
Oven temperature: moderately hot (200°C, 400°F, Gas Mark 6)

METRIC/IMPERIAL
For the batter:
  illustrated recipe, page 34
250 g/9 oz flour
2 tablespoons sugar
½ teaspoon salt
1 tablespoon oil
250 ml/8 fl oz milk
250 ml/8 fl oz water
2 eggs
For the filling:
6 dessert apples
50 g/2 oz butter
3 tablespoons sugar
4 tablespoons double cream
6 tablespoons calvados sweetened with
  1 tablespoon sugar

AMERICAN
For the pancake batter:
  illustrated recipe, page 34
2¼ cups flour
3 tablespoons sugar
½ teaspoon salt
1 tablespoon oil
1 cup milk
1 cup water
2 eggs
For the filling:
6 dessert apples
¼ cup butter
¼ cup sugar
⅓ cup heavy cream
½ cup calvados sweetened with 1
  tablespoon sugar

Prepare a basic pancake batter (see page 34) and if possible leave to stand for 2 hours.

Cook the pancakes in the usual way, cover and keep hot.

Prepare the 'Normandy' filling. Peel, core and thinly slice the apples. Fry them in hot butter for about 10 minutes. When soft and pale brown in colour, add the sugar and cream. Remove from the heat and stir well.

Spread some of the apple filling on each pancake and roll up. Arrange the pancakes on an ovenproof dish.

Reheat for 5 minutes in a moderately hot oven, sprinkle with the sweetened calvados and flambé.

Makes 15-18 pancakes

NOTE The pancakes can be flavoured and flambéed with other spirits, rum for example.

Apple slices

Preparation time: 15 minutes
Cooking time: 30 minutes
Oven temperature: hot (230°C, 450°F, Gas Mark 8)

METRIC/IMPERIAL
4 thick slices slightly stale farmhouse
  bread
50 g/2 oz butter
4 dessert apples
100 g/4 oz sugar

AMERICAN
4 thick slices slightly stale farmhouse
  bread
$\frac{1}{4}$ cup butter
4 dessert apples
$\frac{1}{2}$ cup sugar

Butter the slices of bread. Place them flat on a buttered ovenproof dish, buttered sides uppermost.

Peel the apples and slice thickly. Place a layer of apple on each slice of bread and sprinkle with sugar. Add a second layer of apples and sprinkle with the remaining sugar. Cut the butter into pieces and dot over the apples.

Bake in a hot oven for 30 minutes. The apple slices should brown and become slightly caramelised.

Serves 4

Country cake

Preparation time: 15 minutes
Cooking time: 30–40 minutes
Oven temperature: moderately hot (190°C, 375°F, Gas Mark 5)

METRIC/IMPERIAL	AMERICAN
3 dessert apples	3 dessert apples
juice of 1 lemon	juice of 1 lemon
2 eggs	2 eggs
50 g/2 oz sugar	$\frac{1}{4}$ cup sugar
pinch of salt	dash of salt
50 g/2 oz flour	$\frac{1}{2}$ cup flour
50 g/2 oz butter, melted	$\frac{1}{4}$ cup melted butter
For the caramel:	*For the caramel:*
125 g/5 oz cube sugar	5 oz cube sugar
3 tablespoons water	$\frac{1}{4}$ cup water

To make the caramel, place the sugar cubes in a saucepan and moisten with the water. Dissolve the sugar over a low heat until a light caramel is formed.

Grease the sides of a 20-cm/8-inch cake tin. Coat the base of the tin with the caramel and leave to cool.

Peel, core and thinly slice the apples. Sprinkle with the lemon juice.

Mix the eggs with the sugar and salt in a bowl and beat until the mixture becomes pale and creamy. Then fold in the flour and melted butter alternately in small quantities.

Carefully arrange the apples on the cooled caramel in 2 or 3 layers (when placing the first layer on the caramel arrange the apples neatly as they will form the top of the cake when turned out of the tin).

Pour the cake mixture over the apples.

Bake in a moderately hot oven for 30–40 minutes and turn out of the tin immediately. Serve hot or cold.

Serves 6

Rouen omelette

Preparation time: 15 minutes
Cooking time: 10 minutes for the apples; 10 minutes for the omelette

METRIC/IMPERIAL
2 large cooking apples
100 g/4 oz butter
100 g/4 oz sugar
2 tablespoons double cream
2 tablespoons calvados or rum
5 eggs
pinch of salt

AMERICAN
2 large baking apples
½ cup butter
½ cup sugar
3 tablespoons heavy cream
3 tablespoons calvados or rum
5 eggs
dash of salt

Peel, core and slice the apples and cook in half the butter, turning frequently. Remove from the heat and add 2 tablespoons (U.S. 3 tablespoons) of the sugar, the cream and the calvados. Stir well.

Separate 2 of the eggs and whisk the 2 whites until stiff.

Beat together the yolks and the remaining whole eggs. Add a pinch of salt and 1 tablespoon sugar. Then gently fold in the whisked egg whites.

In a frying pan melt the remaining butter. When light brown in colour pour in the eggs and cook over a moderate heat like an ordinary omelette. Bring the edges towards the centre with a spatula to allow the uncooked egg to run on to the hot pan. This omelette, like all sweet omelettes, should be well cooked and not runny.

When the eggs are firm, spread the apple mixture over the top, fold the omelette in half and slide on to a warmed dish. Sprinkle with the rest of the sugar.

The sugar may be caramelised by placing the omelette under a very hot grill for a few minutes.

If this omelette is not intended for children it can be flambéed.

Serves 4

VARIATION
Other fruits, such as cherries, plums or apricots, can be used for the filling according to the time of year. The flavouring should complement the fruit. Allow 450 g/1 lb of fruit before stoning.

Old fashioned apple flan

Preparation time: 1 hour
Cooking time: 40 minutes
Oven temperature: moderately hot (200°C, 400°F, Gas Mark 6)

METRIC/IMPERIAL
For the filling :
75 g/3 oz raisins
2 tablespoons rum
1 kg/2 lb cooking apples
75 g/3 oz butter
200 g/7 oz castor sugar
1 (28-g/1-oz) sachet vanilla sugar
beaten egg for glazing
For the pâte brisée : illustrated
  recipe, page 28
200 g/7 oz flour
100 g/3½ oz butter
½ teaspoon salt
1 tablespoon sugar
3 tablespoons water

AMERICAN
For the filling :
½ cup raisins
3 tablespoons rum
2 lb baking apples
6 tablespoons butter
scant cup sugar
1 (1-oz) envelope vanilla sugar
beaten egg for glazing
For the pâte brisée : illustrated
  recipe, page 28
1¾ cups flour
scant ½ cup butter
½ teaspoon salt
1 tablespoon sugar
¼ cup water

Soak the raisins in the rum for at least 15 minutes.

Peel, core and slice the apples.

Melt the butter in a frying pan. When light brown in colour, add the apples, sugar and vanilla sugar. Cook for a few minutes and finally add the raisins steeped in rum. Cook carefully over a moderate heat, stirring continuously. The apples should form a lightly caramelised stewed mixture. Leave to cool.

Make the pâte brisée (see page 28) and leave to stand for 30 minutes.

Line a 23-cm/9-inch greased and floured flan tin with three-quarters of the pastry. Fill the case with the cold stewed apple.

Roll out the remaining pastry and cut into 5-mm/¼-inch strips. Decorate the top of the flan with the pastry strips to form a criss-cross pattern. Glaze the pastry lattice work with beaten egg.

Bake in a moderately hot oven for about 40 minutes. Lift out of the tin on to a cooling tray and leave to cool.

Serves 6

Irish flan

Preparation time: 30 minutes
Cooking time: 35-40 minutes for the pastry; 15 minutes for the apples
Oven temperature: moderately hot (200°C, 400°F, Gas Mark 6) reducing
** to moderate (180°C, 350°F, Gas Mark 4)**

METRIC/IMPERIAL	AMERICAN
For the pâte brisée : illustrated recipe, page 28	*For the pâte brisée :* illustrated recipe, page 28
150 g/5 oz flour	1¼ cups flour
75 g/2½ oz butter	5 tablespoons butter
pinch of salt	dash of salt
1 tablespoon sugar	1 tablespoon sugar
2 tablespoons water	3 tablespoons water
For the filling :	*For the filling :*
1 kg/2 lb cooking apples	2 lb baking apples
50 g/2 oz butter	¼ cup butter
100 g/4 oz soft brown sugar	½ cup soft brown sugar
½ teaspoon cinnamon	½ teaspoon cinnamon
1 tablespoon Irish whiskey	1 tablespoon Irish whiskey
3 tablespoons water	¼ cup water
To flambé :	*To flambé :*
2 tablespoons soft brown sugar	3 tablespoons soft brown sugar
½ teaspoon cinnamon	½ teaspoon cinnamon
6 tablespoons whiskey	½ cup whiskey
To serve :	*To serve :*
300 ml/½ pint double cream, whipped	1¼ cups heavy whipped cream

Make the pâte brisée (see page 28) and leave to stand for 30 minutes. Line a 20-cm/8-inch flan tin. Bake blind in a moderately hot oven for 15–20 minutes, remove the beans and reduce the heat to moderate for a further 10–15 minutes.

Peel and core the apples and cut each into 8 thick slices.

Melt the butter in a frying pan and brown the apple slices without crushing them. Add the sugar, cinnamon, whiskey and water. Cover the pan and leave to cook gently until the apples are tender.

Arrange the apple slices neatly in the cooked pastry case. Sprinkle with the brown sugar and cinnamon. Keep hot.

Just before serving warm the whiskey, pour over the apples and flambé. Serve with a jug of whipped cream.

Serves 6

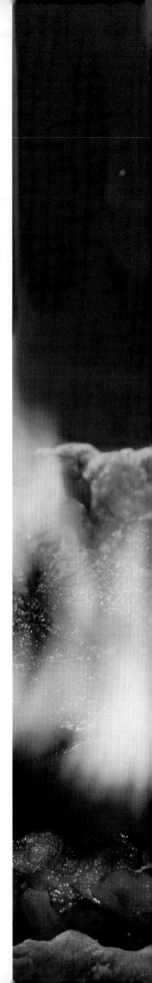

Apricot mousse with raspberries

Preparation time: 20 minutes, plus 3 hours chilling time

METRIC/IMPERIAL
1 kg/2 lb ripe apricots
250 g/12 oz castor sugar
4 leaves gelatine or 15 g/½ oz powdered
  gelatine
150 ml/¼ pint double cream
350 g/12 oz raspberries

AMERICAN
2 lb ripe apricots
1½ cups superfine sugar, finely packed
4 leaves gelatin or 2 envelopes gelatin

⅔ cup heavy cream
¾ lb raspberries

Wash and stone the apricots and reduce to a purée. Sieve to remove any remaining skins.

Add 225 g/8 oz (U.S. 1 cup) sugar.

Soften the leaf gelatine in cold water to cover for about 1 hour, then dissolve it in 2–3 tablespoons (U.S. ¼ cup) hot water. Strain through a fine sieve and add to the puréed apricots, stirring rapidly. If using powdered gelatine, soften it in 2–3 tablespoons (U.S. ¼ cup) cold water and stand the bowl over a pan of hot water to dissolve it. Add to the puréed apricots.

Fold in the whipped cream. Cover the base of a charlotte mould with greaseproof paper and pour in the mixture. Put into the ice-making compartment of the refrigerator for 2–3 hours.

Keep some raspberries for decoration and crush the rest. Mix the remaining sugar into the resulting purée. Keep cool.

To serve Stand the mould in lukewarm water for 20 seconds, wipe and turn out on to a dish. Remove the paper.

Surround the apricot mousse with the raspberry purée and decorate with a few whole raspberries.

Serves 6

Alsace apricots

Preparation time: 10 minutes
Cooking time: 30 minutes (20 minutes, plus 10 minutes under the grill)

METRIC/IMPERIAL
750 g/1¾ lb ripe apricots
6 tablespoons water
250 g/9 oz castor sugar
4 tablespoons kirsch

AMERICAN
1¾ lb ripe apricots
½ cup water
1 cup plus 2 tablespoons superfine sugar
⅓ cup kirsch

Stone the apricots and arrange the halves in the bottom of a flameproof dish, cut side up. Add the water and sprinkle with about two-thirds of the sugar.

Cook over a gentle heat, stirring carefully from time to time.

When the apricots are cooked (there should be very little syrup in the bottom of the dish), sprinkle them with the remaining sugar. Pour the kirsch round the apricots and grill to caramelise the surface.

Carefully transfer the apricots to a glass serving dish or serve directly from the dish they were cooked in.

Serve immediately.

Serves 6

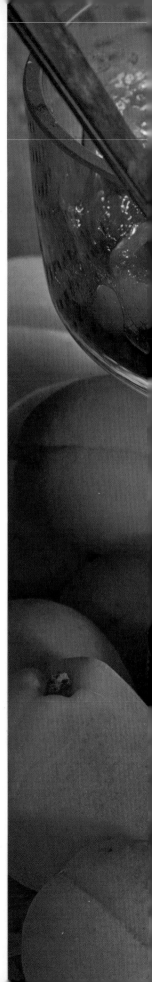

Austrian pudding

Preparation time: 45 minutes, plus 1 hour standing time
Cooking time: 40 minutes
Oven temperature: moderately hot (200°C, 400°F, Gas Mark 6)

METRIC/IMPERIAL
For the pastry:
1 teaspoon dried yeast
3 tablespoons lukewarm milk
250 g/9 oz flour
3 tablespoons cooking oil
50 g/2 oz butter, melted
1 egg
pinch of salt
1 tablespoon sugar
For the decoration:
450 g/1 lb ripe apricots
100 g/4 oz butter
100 g/4 oz flour
200 g/7 oz sugar
1 (28-g/1-oz) sachet vanilla sugar
75 g/3 oz ground almonds
double cream

AMERICAN
For the dough:
1 teaspoon active dry yeast
¼ cup lukewarm milk
2¼ cups flour
¼ cup cooking oil
¼ cup melted butter
1 egg
dash of salt
1 tablespoon sugar
For the decoration:
1 lb ripe apricots
½ cup butter
1 cup flour
scant cup sugar
1 (1-oz) envelope vanilla sugar
¾ cup ground almonds
heavy cream

Dissolve the yeast in the milk. Place the flour in a mixing bowl, form a well and into it pour the oil, melted butter and the yeast liquid, which should be just warm, the egg, salt and sugar.

Mix the ingredients together to form a uniform dough. Knead lightly into a ball, cover and leave to stand in a warm place for about an hour.

Meanwhile prepare the decoration. Wash, dry, stone and halve the apricots. Rub the butter into the flour to form small crumbs, then mix in the sugar, vanilla sugar and ground almonds.

When the original dough has risen and the surface cracked, knead lightly then press it with your hand into the base of a well-buttered, loose-bottomed baking tin 20 cm/8 inches in diameter.

Arrange the apricots on the dough and cover completely with the almond crumble mixture. Cook in a moderately hot oven for 40 minutes.

Serve warm, preferably with double cream.

Serves 8-10

Chilled apricot layer

Preparation time: 30 minutes, plus 24 hours chilling time (very important)

METRIC/IMPERIAL
100 g/4 oz candied lemon peel
2 tablespoons rum
100 g/4 oz raisins
675 g/1½ lb ripe apricots
350 g/12 oz castor sugar
juice of 1 lemon
42 sponge fingers
For the syrup:
3 tablespoons water
4 tablespoons sugar
4 tablespoons rum

AMERICAN
¾ cup candied lemon peel
3 tablespoons rum
¾ cup raisins
1½ lb ripe apricots
1½ cups superfine sugar
juice of 1 lemon
42 lady fingers
For the syrup:
¼ cup water
⅓ cup sugar
⅓ cup rum

Cut the candied lemon peel into small pieces and steep in the rum with the raisins.

Wash and stone the apricots. Purée and sieve to remove any remaining skins. Add the sugar and lemon juice. Stir to completely dissolve the sugar.

To make the syrup Mix the water, sugar and rum in a flat dish. Dip a third of the sponge fingers in the syrup one at a time and place them in the base of an 18-cm/7-inch square cake tin. Sprinkle over half the candied lemon peel and raisins and pour over about a quarter of the apricot purée. Dip another third of the sponge fingers in syrup, place on top of the first layer, sprinkle over the remaining fruit and pour over another quarter of the purée. Dip the remaining sponge fingers in syrup and arrange in a final layer.

Place in the ice-making compartment of the refrigerator for about 3 hours, then place on one of the shelves and allow to stand until the next day. The sponge fingers should be well-soaked in apricot purée.

To serve Remove from the mould and pour the rest of the apricot purée over.

Serves 8

NOTE Out of season this cake can be made with canned or dried apricots.

Apricot condé

Preparation time: about 30 minutes
Cooking time: 45 minutes for the rice, plus 15 minutes in the oven
Oven temperature: moderately hot (200°C, 400°F, Gas Mark 6)

METRIC/IMPERIAL
200 g/7 oz round-grain rice
1 litre/1¾ pints milk
1 vanilla pod
pinch of salt
150 g/5 oz sugar
3 eggs, beaten
3 tablespoons double cream
For the decoration:
1 (822-g/1 lb 13-oz) can apricots in
 syrup
glacé cherries and angelica
25 g/1 oz sugar
3 tablespoons rum or kirsch

AMERICAN
scant cup round-grain rice
4¼ cups milk
1 vanilla bean
dash of salt
⅔ cup sugar, firmly packed
3 eggs, beaten
¼ cup heavy cream
For the decoration:
1 (29-oz) can apricots in syrup

candied cherries and angelica
2 tablespoons sugar
¼ cup rum or kirsch

Wash the rice and plunge it for 2 minutes into a large pan of boiling water, then drain. Bring the milk to the boil together with the vanilla pod. Allow to stand for 5 minutes. Remove the vanilla pod then add the rice and a pinch of salt. Bring to the boil then reduce the heat. Cover and leave to cook over a very low heat for about 45 minutes.

Add the sugar, beaten eggs and cream to the cooked rice. Pour into a buttered 20-cm/8-inch round or hexagonal crown mould, stand in a bain marie and finish

cooking in the oven for 15 minutes. Allow to cool and set.

Pick out the twelve best apricot halves from the can. Heat them in a dish standing in the bain marie. Crush the rest to form a purée and add several drops of rum. Heat gently.

To serve Turn out the rice on to a plate and pour the apricot purée over the top. In the centre of the crown place the warmed apricot halves. Decorate with the cherries and angelica, sprinkle over the sugar, then sprinkle with rum and flambé.

Serves 6

VARIATION
Condé with Pineapple and Strawberries 1 (376-g/13¼-oz) can pineapple in syrup, 225 g/8 oz strawberries, 225 g/8 oz (U.S. ⅔ cup) apricot jam, 3 tablespoons (U.S. ¼ cup) rum or kirsch.

Proceed as for the Apricot Condé.

For the decoration Cut the pineapple rings into even pieces. Warm through over a low heat in a little of their syrup. Sieve the

apricot jam and if necessary make it a little more liquid by adding a few spoonfuls of syrup.

Turn the rice out of the mould and top with apricot sauce. Place the pieces of pineapple in the centre of the crown. Wash and hull the strawberries and use to decorate. Sprinkle with sugar and liqueur and flambé.

Apricot upside-down pudding

Preparation time: 20 minutes
Cooking time: 5–10 minutes on the burner, plus 25–30 minutes baking time
Oven temperature: hot (220°C, 425°F, Gas Mark 7)

METRIC/IMPERIAL

For the pâte brisée: illustrated recipe,
  page 28
150 g/5 oz flour
75 g/2½ oz butter
½ teaspoon salt
1 teaspoon sugar
1 tablespoon water
For the caramel: illustrated recipe,
  page 38
100 g/4 oz cube sugar
3–4 tablespoons water
For the filling:
675 g/1½ lb apricots
100 g/4 oz sugar
25 g/1 oz butter

AMERICAN

For the pâte brisée: illustrated recipe,
  page 28
1¼ cups flour
5 tablespoons butter
½ teaspoon salt
1 teaspoon sugar
1 tablespoon water
For the caramel: illustrated recipe,
  page 38
¼ lb cube sugar
¼–⅓ cup water
For the filling:
1½ lb apricots
½ cup sugar
2 tablespoons butter

First prepare the pastry (see page 28) and leave to stand for 20 minutes.

Make a dark caramel with the sugar and water. Coat the base and about 3.5 cm/1½ inches of the sides of a 20-cm/8-inch round cake tin with this caramel. Allow to cool slightly.

Halve and stone the apricots and place an even layer in the tin, rounded sides on the caramel. Cut the rest of the apricots into pieces and arrange over the halves.

Sprinkle the sugar over the fruit and dot with the butter.

Roll out the pastry to a round slightly larger than the tin then cover the fruit with it, pushing the pastry down at the edges to reach the base of the tin. Cook in a hot oven for 25–30 minutes. The pastry should be well browned.

Turn out of the tin immediately on removing from the oven. Serve hot or cold.

Serves 6

NOTE This recipe can be made similarly with plums or apples.

Martinique bananas

Preparation and cooking time: 20 minutes

METRIC/IMPERIAL
2 oranges
50 g/2 oz raisins
50 g/2 oz sugar
1 (28-g/1-oz) sachet vanilla sugar
6 bananas
50 g/2 oz butter
6 tablespoons rum

AMERICAN
2 oranges
⅓ cup raisins
¼ cup sugar
1 (1-oz) envelope vanilla sugar
6 bananas
¼ cup butter
½ cup rum

This dish should be cooked immediately before serving.

Squeeze the juice of the oranges. Wash the raisins. Mix the sugar and vanilla sugar. Peel the bananas.

Warm the serving dish and get out a frying pan, a palette knife for turning the fruit and a spoon for basting. At the last moment heat the butter in the frying pan, cook the bananas for 4 or 5 minutes on each side until golden.

Add the sugar, orange juice and raisins. Bring to the boil, add half the rum and simmer for 5 minutes more.

Arrange on the hot serving dish. Warm the rest of the rum in a small saucepan. Flambé at the table and pour over the fruit while still flaming.

For children, omit the rum, or serve the bananas before flambéeing.

Serves 6

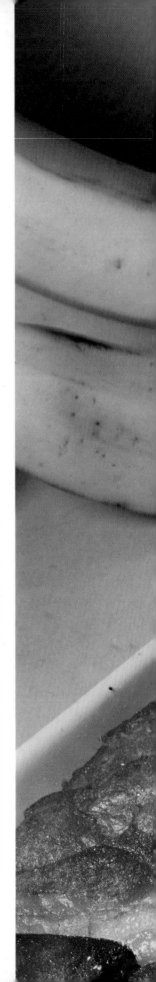

Creole fritters

Preparation time: 30 minutes, plus 30 minutes standing for the butter
Cooking time: 2–3 minutes

METRIC/IMPERIAL
4 bananas
juice of ½ lemon
50 g/2 oz sugar
2 tablespoons rum
1 litre/1¾ pints oil for frying
50 g/2 oz icing sugar
3 tablespoons rum for flambéeing
  (optional)
For the fritter batter:
1 teaspoon dried yeast
6 tablespoons lukewarm milk
100 g/4 oz flour
50 g/2 oz cornflour
1 tablespoon sugar
1 (28-g/1-oz) sachet vanilla sugar
pinch of salt
1 large egg
1 tablespoon oil

AMERICAN
4 bananas
juice of ½ lemon
¼ cup sugar
3 tablespoons rum
4¼ cups oil for frying
½ cup confectioners' sugar
¼ cup rum for flambéeing (optional)
For the fritter batter:
1 teaspoon active dry yeast
½ cup lukewarm milk
1 cup flour
⅓ cup cornstarch
1 tablespoon sugar
1 (1-oz) envelope vanilla sugar
dash of salt
1 large egg
1 tablespoon oil

Peel the bananas and cut in two lengthways. Put to steep in the lemon juice, sugar and rum.

Prepare the fritter batter. Dissolve the yeast in the warmed milk. In a mixing bowl, mix together the flour, cornflour, sugar, vanilla sugar and salt. Form a well and into it put the egg, oil and yeast liquid and gradually work in to obtain a batter, smooth and thick but still runny.

Serves 6-8

NOTE Pineapple or apples can also be used for this recipe.

Leave in a warm place for 30 minutes.

Heat the oil to 170°C/340°F. Drain the bananas and dip into the batter which should cover them completely. Place in the hot oil.

When the fritters are golden brown, drain on kitchen paper and arrange on a hot dish. Sprinkle with icing sugar. If desired, sprinkle with warm rum and flambé.

Caramelita

Preparation time: 20 minutes
Cooking time: 7–8 minutes, plus 7–8 minutes for the caramel

METRIC/IMPERIAL
For the cream:
750 ml/1¼ pints milk
250 g/9 oz castor sugar
1 vanilla pod, pierced
4 eggs
1 tablespoon cornflour
For the caramel: illustrated recipe,
    page 38
50 g/2 oz cube sugar
1 tablespoon warm water
½ teaspoon lemon juice

AMERICAN
For the cream:
3 cups milk
1 cup plus 2 tablespoons sugar
1 vanilla bean, pierced
4 eggs
1 tablespoon cornstarch
For the caramel: illustrated recipe,
    page 38
2 oz cube sugar
1 tablespoon warm water
½ teaspoon lemon juice

Bring the milk to the boil with 150 g/5 oz (U.S. ⅔ cup) castor sugar and the vanilla pod.

Separate the eggs and keep the whites to one side.

Stir the cornflour into the egg yolks. Gradually add the hot milk, stirring continuously. Replace the mixture on the stove, stirring continuously until the mix-

ture thickens. Pour into a heatproof glass bowl.

Whisk the egg whites until stiff, sprinkle with the remaining 100 g/4 oz (U.S. ½ cup) castor sugar and whisk for several minutes until smooth and shiny.

Spoon the meringue over the hot cream without stirring.

Top with a light caramel.

Serves 6

NOTE On the same principle you can prepare 'snowy eggs' by poaching the whites for a few moments in boiling water.

South Sea sorbet

Preparation time: 15 minutes, plus about 3 hours setting time

METRIC/IMPERIAL
4 bananas, crushed
300 ml/½ pint orange juice
150 ml/¼ pint lemon juice
250 g/9 oz castor sugar
1 egg white

AMERICAN
4 bananas, crushed
1¼ cups orange juice
⅔ cup lemon juice
1 cup plus 2 tablespoons superfine sugar
1 egg white

Mix the crushed bananas, orange and lemon juice and sugar. Leave in a freezer box in the ice-making compartment of the refrigerator until half frozen, about 2–3 hours.

Whisk the egg white until stiff. Beat the banana mixture and carefully fold in the whisked egg white. Put back in the ice-making compartment to set.

Serve the sorbet cut into cubes in glasses.

Serves 4

VARIATION
This sorbet can be made with other more exotic fruits.

Reduce 2 ripe papaws and 2 bananas to a purée, preferably in a liquidiser to give a smooth purée. Add the juice of 2 limes and 150 g/5 oz (U.S. ⅔ cup) castor sugar. Leave to set.

Easter caramel mousse

Preparation time: 30 minutes. Make 1 day in advance
Cooking time: 7–8 minutes for the caramel; 7–8 minutes for the mousse

METRIC/IMPERIAL
2 leaves gelatine or 7 g/¼ oz powdered
  gelatine
6 egg whites
50 g/2 oz sugar
150 g/5 oz small sugar-coated eggs
For the caramel: illustrated recipe,
  page 38
150 g/5 oz cube sugar
3 tablespoons water
For the custard: illustrated recipe,
  page 22
1 litre/1¾ pints milk
1 vanilla pod, pierced
6 egg yolks
125 g/4½ oz sugar

AMERICAN
2 leaves gelatin or 1 envelope
  gelatin
6 egg whites
¼ cup sugar
5 oz small sugar-coated eggs
For the caramel: illustrated recipe,
  page 38
5 oz cube sugar
¼ cup water
For the custard: illustrated recipe,
  page 22
4¼ cups milk
1 vanilla bean, pierced
6 egg yolks
generous ½ cup sugar

Soften the leaf gelatine in cold water to cover for about 1 hour then dissolve it in 2 tablespoons (U.S. 3 tablespoons) hot water. Keep hot. If using powdered gelatine, soften it in 2 tablespoons (U.S. 3 tablespoons) cold water and stand the bowl over a pan of hot water to dissolve it.

Dissolve the sugar cubes in the water over low heat, then bring to the boil and cook until a deep golden brown caramel is obtained.

When the caramel is almost ready, whisk the egg whites until stiff in a fairly large bowl. Sprinkle the 50 g/2 oz (U.S. ¼ cup) sugar over the surface and pour in the dissolved gelatine. Pour the caramel in a slow stream on to the side of the dish containing the egg whites, whisking the whites with a hand whisk. The eggs will cook in the heat from the caramel.

Leave the mousse until just warm and gently stir in half the sugar-coated eggs.

Pour into a moist 18-cm/7-inch charlotte mould and leave to stand in the refrigerator overnight.

To make the vanilla custard Bring the milk to the boil with the vanilla pod. Work together the egg yolks and sugar and pour the boiling milk (with the vanilla pod removed) into this mixture. Thicken in a bowl over a saucepan of boiling water, stirring continuously. The custard is ready when it will coat a spoon. Leave to cool and keep in the refrigerator.

To turn out the mousse from the mould, run a knife around the edge. Dip the base of the mould into hot water for 10 seconds. Dry and turn out the mousse into the centre of the serving dish. It will come free after a few seconds.

Pour the custard around it and arrange the rest of the sugar-coated eggs on top.

Serves 6

86

Quebec sugar flan

Preparation time: 30 minutes
Cooking time: 30 minutes
Oven temperature: moderately hot (200°C, 400°F, Gas Mark 6)

METRIC/IMPERIAL
½ teaspoon dried yeast
3–4 tablespoons lukewarm water
125 g/4½ oz butter
250 g/9 oz flour
50 g/2 oz sugar
1 egg
½ teaspoon salt
For the filling:
250 g/9 oz demerara, or light or dark
  soft brown sugar, or a mixture of
  the two
250 ml/8 fl oz double cream
100 g/4 oz chopped walnuts

AMERICAN
½ teaspoon active dry yeast
¼–⅓ cup lukewarm water
generous ½ cup butter
2¼ cups flour
¼ cup sugar
1 egg
½ teaspoon salt
For the filling:
1 cup plus 2 tablespoons light or dark
  soft brown sugar, or a mixture of the
  two
1 cup heavy cream
1 cup chopped walnuts

Dissolve the yeast in the water and leave to stand in a warm place for a few minutes. Rub the butter into the flour until it resembles breadcrumbs. Mix in the sugar. Make a well in the centre and put in it the egg, salt and yeast liquid. Work all the ingredients together and form into a ball.

Leave to stand for 30 minutes in the refrigerator to become firmer.

Roll the pastry out to 5 mm/¼ inch thickness and line a lightly greased 25-cm/10-inch flan tin. Bake blind for 10 minutes.

To make the filling In a saucepan slowly bring the brown sugar and the cream to the boil. Remove from the heat immediately and add the chopped nuts. Leave to cool.

Fill the flan case and bake in a moderately hot oven for 30 minutes.

Remove from the flan tin and leave to cool.

Serves 6-8

Clafoutis

Preparation time: 15 minutes
Cooking time: 35-45 minutes
Oven temperature: moderately hot (200°C, 400°F, Gas Mark 6)

METRIC/IMPERIAL	AMERICAN
75 g/3 oz flour	¾ cup flour
50 g/2 oz sugar	¼ cup sugar
pinch of salt	dash of salt
3 eggs	3 eggs
450 ml/¾ pint milk	2 cups milk
450 g/1 lb black cherries	1 lb Bing cherries
25 g/1 oz butter	2 tablespoons butter
castor sugar for sprinkling	sugar for sprinkling

Sift the flour into a mixing bowl. Make a well in the centre and in it put the sugar, salt and eggs. Gradually stir in the flour. When the mixture thickens add the milk a little at a time. You should obtain quite a runny batter without lumps.

Wash the cherries and remove the stalks and stones.

Thoroughly grease a large, shallow, oval dish with the butter (the dish should be stainless steel or ovenproof porcelain).

Serves 4–6

NOTE The dessert can be made with apricots, pears, apples, plums or prunes and even with pineapple or bananas.

Spread the cherries over the base. Gently pour on the batter. If you have a little butter left over, use it to dot the surface.

Place in the centre of a moderately hot oven and cook for 35–45 minutes. During cooking the cherries will spread throughout the sponge which rises and browns. It will fall when cool.

Sprinkle with sugar before serving either hot or cold.

Itxassou basque cake

Preparation time: 30 minutes
Cooking time: 1¼ hours
Oven temperature: moderately hot (190°C, 375°F, Gas Mark 5) reducing
 to moderate (160°C, 325°F, Gas Mark 3)

METRIC/IMPERIAL	AMERICAN
275 g/10 oz flour	2½ cups flour
200 g/7 oz sugar	scant cup sugar
1 whole egg	1 whole egg
2 egg yolks	2 egg yolks
pinch of salt	dash of salt
200 g/7 oz butter	¾ cup plus 2 tablespoons butter
grated rind of 1 lemon	grated rind of 1 lemon
450 g/1 lb cherry jam	1 lb cherry jam

Sift the flour into a mixing bowl. Make a well in the centre and in it put the sugar, the whole egg and the egg yolks (keeping a little to brush over the cake) and a pinch of salt.

Beginning at the centre, stir with a wooden spoon to begin mixing the ingredients. Then continue to knead with the hands, working in the butter which should be cut into small pieces. Flavour the dough with a little grated lemon rind. When the dough has a smooth consistency, form into a ball and leave to stand in the bottom of the refrigerator for about 1 hour.

Take two-thirds of the dough and with your hand spread it over the base and sides of a lined and greased 21-cm/8½-inch sandwich tin. Fill the hollow with the cherry jam.

Roll out the rest of the dough and cover the cake. Seal the edges well so that the jam does not run out. Pierce the lid several times with the point of a knife.

Score the surface and brush with the egg yolk which was kept back for this purpose. Bake in a moderately hot oven for about 45 minutes, then reduce the temperature and cook for a further 30 minutes. Leave to cool before removing from the tin.

Serves 8

VARIATION
Basque cake is sometimes filled with crème pâtissière (illustrated recipe, page 23) flavoured with rum instead of the cherry jam.

Prepare the cream in advance so that it has time to cool before being poured into the pastry:

2 egg yolks, 50 g/2 oz (U.S. ¼ cup) sugar, 25 g/1 oz (U.S. ¼ cup) flour, 250 ml/8 fl oz (U.S. 1 cup) milk, 1 tablespoon rum.

Finish off the cake by proceeding in exactly the same way, simply replacing the jam with the cream.

Chocolate and cherry gâteau

Preparation time: 50 minutes
Cooking time: 25 minutes
Oven temperature: moderate (180°C, 350°F, Gas Mark 4)

METRIC/IMPERIAL
50 g/2 oz butter
6 eggs
1 teaspoon vanilla essence
175 g/6 oz sugar
50 g/2 oz flour, sifted
75 g/3 oz cocoa powder
For the syrup:
180 g/6½ oz sugar
300 ml/½ pint cold water
3 tablespoons kirsch
For the filling:
750 ml/1¼ pints double cream
4 tablespoons kirsch
450 g/1 lb stoned cherries (or liqueur
  cherries, drained and rinsed)
For the chocolate flakes: see
  Christmas Log, page 116
225 g/8 oz plain chocolate
few whole cherries for decoration

AMERICAN
¼ cup butter
6 eggs
1 teaspoon vanilla extract
¾ cup sugar
½ cup sifted flour
¾ cup cocoa powder
For the syrup:
generous ¾ cup sugar
1¼ cups cold water
¼ cup kirsch
For the filling:
3 cups heavy cream
⅓ cup kirsch
1 lb pitted cherries (or liqueur cherries,
  drained and rinsed)
For the chocolate flakes: see
  Christmas Log, page 116
8 squares semi-sweet chocolate
few whole cherries for decoration

Preheat the oven.

Melt the butter over a low heat.

Place the eggs, vanilla and sugar in a mixer and beat at a high speed setting for 10 minutes to obtain a thick, creamy mixture.

Sift the flour and cocoa powder a little at a time into the bowl containing the eggs. Fold in with a spatula and slowly add the melted butter. Do not over-stir.

Divide this mixture into three greased and floured sandwich tins 20 cm/8 inches in diameter.

Bake for about 25 minutes. Leave to stand for 5 minutes before removing from the tins.

Meanwhile prepare the syrup. Bring the sugar and water to the boil, stirring continuously. Add the stoned cherries and poach gently for 5 minutes. Drain and allow the syrup to cool, then flavour with kirsch. Pierce the top of the three cakes and pour over the syrup.

Whisk the cream, which should be very cold, in a large bowl until it is thick. Stir in the kirsch.

Place one of the cakes on a large serving dish, cover with a layer of cream 1 cm/½ inch thick and sprinkle with half the poached cherries, leaving a border of 1 cm/½ inch around the cherries. Gently place the second cake on top and cover with a layer of cream and the remaining cherries, then add the third cake.

Cover the top and sides of the cake with the rest of the cream and press the chocolate flakes around the sides. Decorate with whole cherries.

Serves 8–10

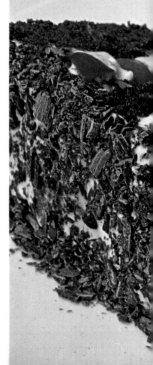

Cherry flan

Preparation time: 40 minutes
Cooking time: 1 hour
Oven temperature: moderately hot (200°C, 400°F, Gas Mark 6)

METRIC/IMPERIAL

For the pâte brisée : illustrated recipe,
  page 28
100 g/3½ oz butter
200 g/7 oz flour
½ teaspoon salt
1 tablespoon sugar
3 tablespoons water
For the filling :
1 kg/2 lb cherries
75 g/3 oz sugar
200 ml/6 fl oz single cream
100 g/4 oz dry almond macaroons
1 tablespoon kirsch

AMERICAN

For the pâte brisée : illustrated recipe,
  page 28
scant ½ cup butter
1¾ cups flour
½ teaspoon salt
1 tablespoon sugar
¼ cup water
For the filling :
2 lb cherries
6 tablespoons sugar
¾ cup light cream
¼ lb dry almond macaroons
1 tablespoon kirsch

Prepare the pastry (see page 28) and leave to stand in a cool place for 30 minutes. Then roll out the pastry and line a 25-cm/10-inch flan tin.

Wash and stone the cherries and arrange them in the flan case, pressing down well.

Sprinkle with the sugar and bake in a moderately hot oven for 40 minutes. Cover with foil if the flan begins to brown too rapidly.

Top the cherries with cream made as follows:

Crush the macaroons very finely. Stir the cream into the crushed macaroons to give a soft mixture. Spread this mixture over the hot flan and return to the oven for 20 minutes. Leave to cool before removing from the tin.

Serves 8-10

VARIATION
This recipe may also be made with plums.

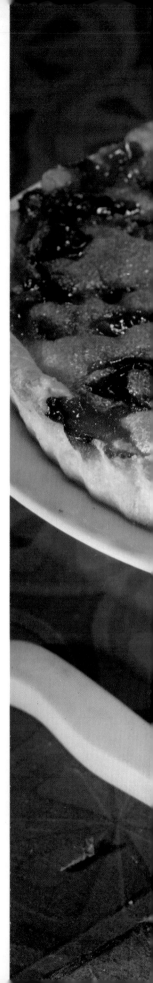

Chestnut bavarois

Preparation time: 30 minutes. May be made 1 day in advance
Chilling time: at least 4–5 hours in the refrigerator

METRIC/IMPERIAL
8 leaves gelatine or 25 g/1 oz powdered
 gelatine
325 ml/11 fl oz milk
1 vanilla pod, pierced
50 g/2 oz sugar
6 egg yolks
250 ml/8 fl oz double cream
1 (880-g/1 lb 15-oz) can unsweetened
 chestnut purée
2 tablespoons kirsch
For the caramel: illustrated recipe,
 page 38
175 g/6 oz cube sugar
6 tablespoons water
For the decoration:
300 ml/½ pint crème Chantilly:
 illustrated recipe, page 25

AMERICAN
8 leaves gelatin or 4 envelopes
 gelatin
1⅓ cups milk
1 vanilla bean, pierced
¼ cup sugar
6 egg yolks
1 cup heavy cream
1 (32-oz) can unsweetened chestnut
 purée
3 tablespoons kirsch
For the caramel: illustrated recipe,
 page 38
6 oz cube sugar
½ cup water
For the decoration:
1¼ cups crème Chantilly:
 illustrated recipe, page 25

If using leaf gelatine, soften it by soaking for 1 hour in cold water.

Prepare a thick custard. Bring the milk to the boil with the vanilla pod. Beat the sugar into the egg yolks. Gradually pour in the hot milk. Thicken over a low heat, stirring continuously. Remove from the heat just before it boils.

Add the softened gelatine to the hot custard. Stir well, then leave until completely cool. Strain the custard to remove any pieces of gelatine that have not dissolved. If using powdered gelatine, soften it in 4 tablespoons (U.S. ⅓ cup) cold water and stand the bowl over a pan of hot water to dissolve it. Stir into the hot custard.

Whip the cream. Stir the chestnut purée and the whipped cream into the custard. Flavour with the kirsch.

In a small saucepan prepare a light caramel with the cube sugar and water (see page 38). Pour into a 21-cm/8½-inch pudding mould (or a cake tin or charlotte mould). Cover the sides evenly by rolling the caramel around them.

Pour the mixture into the mould and leave to stand in the refrigerator for several hours. The dish should set like a jelly.

To remove from the mould, stand the mould in hot water for 30 seconds. Wipe the mould and turn out on to the centre of a plate.

Decorate with piped crème Chantilly and the marrons glacés. Serve at once.

Serves 10–12

Chestnut log

**Preparation time: 30 minutes, plus overnight in the refrigerator or
1–2 hours in the ice-making compartment of the refrigerator**

METRIC/IMPERIAL
125 g/4½ oz plain chocolate
2 tablespoons water
125 g/4½ oz butter
450 g/1 lb chestnut purée
125 g/4½ oz icing sugar

AMERICAN
4½ squares semi-sweet chocolate
3 tablespoons water
generous ½ cup butter
scant 2 cups chestnut purée
1 cup confectioners' sugar

Melt the chocolate in the water in a basin over a saucepan of hot water.

Work the butter with a palette knife to soften it.

Work the chestnut purée until completely free from lumps, add the icing sugar, butter and melted chocolate. Beat the mixture until very smooth and light.

Transfer with a spoon on to foil, form into a roll and leave to chill in a cool place or in the ice-making compartment of the refrigerator.

When the roll is firm, remove the foil and cut the ends slantwise. Place on a dish and form into a log. Make the bark markings with a fork. Decorate with sifted icing sugar, meringue mushrooms, etc. Keep in the refrigerator until required.

Serves 8

Chestnut ice cream

Preparation time: 20 minutes
Freezing time: about 2–3 hours in the ice-making compartment of the refrigerator at the coldest setting

METRIC/IMPERIAL
For the custard: illustrated recipe,
  page 22
4 egg yolks
50 g/2 oz sugar
500 ml/17 fl oz milk
1 vanilla pod, pierced
6 tablespoons double cream
300 g/11 oz chestnut purée
1 tablespoon rum or kirsch
For the decoration:
100 g/4 oz plain chocolate
3 tablespoons milk
6 tablespoons crème Chantilly:
  illustrated recipe, page 25

AMERICAN
For the custard: illustrated recipe,
  page 22
4 egg yolks
¼ cup sugar
1 cup milk
1 vanilla bean, pierced
½ cup heavy cream
1⅓ cups chestnut purée
1 tablespoon rum or kirsch
For the decoration:
4 squares semi-sweet chocolate
¼ cup milk
½ cup crème Chantilly:
  illustrated recipe, page 25

Prepare the custard (see page 22) and leave until quite cold.

Stir the cream, chestnut purée and the rum or kirsch into the custard. Place in an ice cream maker and freeze. If you do not have an ice cream maker, whisk the mixture for 1 or 2 minutes until frothy, then pour this mixture into a freezing container and freeze until half frozen. Remove from the refrigerator and whisk thoroughly, then return to the refrigerator until completely frozen. Melt the chocolate in a basin over a pan of hot water together with the milk. Leave this thick sauce to cool.

Just before serving, form the ice cream into balls, either with a special ice cream scoop or with 2 tablespoons. Place 2 or 3 balls in each individual serving dish.

Top with the cold chocolate sauce and decorate with a little crème Chantilly (see page 25) if liked.

For a Christmas meal this ice cream can form the basis of the filling for a marron glacé meringue, in the same way as the Pineapple vacherin (see page 216).

Serves 6

Ardèche cake

Preparation time: 20 minutes
Cooking time: 35–40 minutes
Oven temperature: moderate (160°C, 325°F, Gas Mark 3)

METRIC/IMPERIAL	AMERICAN
100 g/4 oz butter	$\frac{1}{2}$ cup butter
175 g/6 oz sugar	$\frac{3}{4}$ cup sugar
100 g/4 oz unsweetened chestnut purée	scant $\frac{1}{2}$ cup unsweetened chestnut purée
1 tablespoon instant coffee	1 tablespoon instant coffee
1 tablespoon hot water	1 tablespoon hot water
3 eggs	3 eggs
175 g/6 oz self-raising flour	1$\frac{1}{2}$ cups all-purpose flour sifted with 1$\frac{1}{2}$ teaspoons baking powder

Cream the butter and sugar together until light and fluffy. Beat in the chestnut purée until thoroughly mixed.

Blend the coffee and hot water together, then add to the creamed chestnut mixture. Add the eggs one at a time, adding a little flour with each one.

Fold in the remaining flour.

Place the mixture in a greased and base-lined 20-cm/8-inch sandwich tin. Bake in a moderate oven for 35–40 minutes. Turn out and cool on a wire tray.

Serve with brandy cream or brandy butter.

Serves 6

Chocolate Acropolis

**Preparation time: 30 minutes. Prepare 1 day in advance
Cooking time: 8 minutes**

METRIC/IMPERIAL
150 g/5 oz plain chocolate
50 g/2 oz butter
25 g/1 oz castor sugar
2 tablespoons water
4 eggs, separated
38 sponge fingers
6 tablespoons very strong sweetened
  black coffee
grated chocolate or chocolate vermicelli
  for decoration

AMERICAN
5 squares semi-sweet chocolate
¼ cup butter
2 tablespoons sugar
3 tablespoons water
4 eggs, separated
38 lady fingers
½ cup very strong sweetened black
  coffee
grated chocolate or chocolate sprinkles
  for decoration

Break the chocolate into pieces and place in a bowl together with the butter, sugar and water. Melt over a saucepan of hot water.

When thoroughly melted, stir to form a smooth cream. Remove from the heat and add the egg yolks, stirring well.

Whisk the egg whites until stiff and fold into the chocolate cream. Reserve 1 tablespoon of the mousse for decoration and leave the remaining mousse in a cool place.

Line the base and sides of a 1-kg/2-lb loaf tin with sponge fingers (trimmed to fit the tin), with the rounded sides to the tin.

Then fill the tin with alternate layers of chocolate mousse and sponge fingers dipped individually for 3 or 4 seconds in the sweetened coffee.

Leave overnight in the refrigerator.

Turn out of the tin on to an oblong dish. Spread the cream which was kept back for decoration over the top of the cake and sprinkle with grated chocolate or chocolate vermicelli.

Serves 6

Balthazar

Preparation time: 30 minutes
Cooking time: 25 minutes
**Oven temperature: hot (220°C, 425°F, Gas Mark 7) reducing to
  moderate (180°C, 350°F, Gas Mark 4)**

METRIC/IMPERIAL
150 g/5 oz plain chocolate
25 g/1 oz butter
1 teaspoon dried yeast
1 tablespoon lukewarm rum
3 eggs, separated
75 g/3 oz castor sugar
50 g/1 oz flour, sifted
For the icing:
150 g/5 oz plain chocolate
2 tablespoons water
25 g/1 oz butter
2 tablespoons rum
For the crème Chantilly:
  illustrated recipe, page 25
50 g/2 oz icing sugar
300 ml/½ pint double cream

AMERICAN
5 squares semi-sweet chocolate
2 tablespoons butter
1 teaspoon active dry yeast
1 tablespoon lukewarm rum
3 eggs, separated
6 tablespoons sugar
¼ cup sifted flour
For the frosting:
5 squares semi-sweet chocolate
3 tablespoons water
2 tablespoons butter
3 tablespoons rum
For the crème Chantilly:
  illustrated recipe, page 25
½ cup confectioners' sugar
1¼ cups heavy cream

Break the chocolate into pieces and melt with the butter in a bowl over a saucepan of hot water. Stir to form a smooth cream.

Dissolve the yeast in the lukewarm rum and leave until frothy.

In a basin beat together the egg yolks and sugar. Add the sifted flour and the yeast liquid. Working quickly, carefully fold in the melted chocolate and butter. If the chocolate has time to harden the mixture will become too stiff.

Whisk the egg whites until stiff and gently fold into the mixture.

Thoroughly grease a 23-cm/9-inch ring mould and pour in the mixture. Bake in a hot oven for 10 minutes, then lower the temperature to moderate and bake for a further 15 minutes.

Cool slightly in the tin then turn out on to a wire tray.

To make the icing Melt the chocolate with the water and butter in a bowl over a saucepan of hot water. Add the rum.

Place the cake in the centre of a dish and cover with this icing. Fill the centre with crème Chantilly (see page 25).

Serves 6-8

Chocolate marchioness

Preparation time: 30 minutes, plus 15 minutes for the custard. Make 1 day in advance preferably

METRIC/IMPERIAL
For the chocolate pudding:
250 g/9 oz plain chocolate
3 tablespoons water
125 g/4½ oz butter
3 eggs
100 g/4 oz icing sugar
vanilla or coffee essence
For the custard: illustrated recipe, page 22
2 egg yolks
50 g/2 oz sugar
250 ml/8 fl oz milk
vanilla or coffee essence

AMERICAN
For the chocolate pudding:
9 squares semi-sweet chocolate
¼ cup water
generous ½ cup butter
3 eggs
scant cup confectioners' sugar
vanilla or coffee extract
For the custard: illustrated recipe, page 22
2 egg yolks
¼ cup sugar
1 cup milk
vanilla or coffee extract

Melt the chocolate with the water in a bowl over a saucepan of hot water. When melted, remove from the heat.

Beat the butter until creamy. Do not on any account heat it or its flavour will be lost.

Separate the eggs. Beat the yolks one at a time into the creamy butter. Then add the icing sugar, sifting it if it is lumpy, and beat the cream well.

Mix in the melted chocolate and flavour with vanilla or coffee essence. Beat the mixture well. Leave until completely cool.

Whisk the egg whites until stiff then fold into the chocolate and butter mixture.

Pour into a well-greased 600-ml/1-pint (U.S. 1½-pint) fluted mould. Leave to stand in the refrigerator overnight.

Prepare a vanilla or coffee custard (see page 22) and leave to cool.

To remove the pudding from the mould, dip the mould for a few seconds in hot water. Turn out on to a dish and surround with the custard.

Serves 8–10

Chocolate pots

Preparation time: 20 minutes

METRIC/IMPERIAL
100 g/4 oz plain chocolate
1 tablespoon water
4 eggs, separated
grated rind of 1 orange
100 g/2 oz castor sugar
50 g/2 oz flaked almonds, toasted

AMERICAN
4 squares semi-sweet chocolate
1 tablespoon water
4 eggs, separated
grated rind of 1 orange
$\frac{1}{4}$ cup sugar
$\frac{1}{2}$ cup flaked, toasted almonds

Place the chocolate and water in a small bowl and melt over a saucepan of hot water.

Remove from the heat and beat in the egg yolks. Stir in the grated orange rind.

Whisk the egg whites until very stiff, then whisk in the castor sugar to give a very firm meringue.

Gently fold the two mixtures together. Pour into individual dishes and decorate the tops with the almonds.

Serves 6

VARIATION
This mousse is equally delicious when flavoured with coffee. In this instance, add 1 tablespoon coffee essence instead of the orange rind.

Profiteroles

Preparation time: 15 minutes for the pastry, plus 15 minutes for the cream
Cooking time: 20–30 minutes
Oven temperature: moderately hot (200°C, 400°F, Gas Mark 6)

METRIC/IMPERIAL

For the choux pastry: illustrated recipe, page 35
75 g/3 oz butter
250 ml/8 fl oz water
½ teaspoon salt
1 tablespoon sugar
150 g/5 oz flour, sifted
4 eggs
For the crème Chantilly:
  illustrated recipe, page 25
50 g/2 oz vanilla sugar
250 ml/8 fl oz double cream
For the chocolate sauce:
250 g/9 oz plain chocolate
50 g/2 oz butter
6 tablespoons milk

AMERICAN

For the choux paste: illustrated recipe, page 35
6 tablespoons butter
1 cup water
½ teaspoon salt
1 tablespoon sugar
1¼ cups sifted flour
4 eggs
For the crème Chantilly:
  illustrated recipe, page 25
¼ cup vanilla sugar
1 cup heavy cream
For the chocolate sauce:
9 squares semi-sweet chocolate
¼ cup butter
½ cup milk

Make the choux pastry (see page 35).

Lightly grease a baking sheet and with two teaspoons place small spoonfuls of pastry on to it. Bake in a moderately hot oven until the little choux buns are risen, golden brown and very light – about 20–30 minutes.

Leave to cool, then fill each one with the crème Chantilly (see page 25).

Makes about 30

VARIATION
The recipe can be varied in summer by filling the choux buns with ice cream or whipped cream and topping with raspberry purée.

To make the chocolate sauce Melt the chocolate and butter in the milk in a bowl over a saucepan of hot water.

Arrange the profiteroles on a serving dish and pour over the chocolate sauce while it is still hot.

Profiteroles can also be filled with vanilla ice cream or crème pâtissière (see page 23).

Christmas log

Preparation time: 40 minutes for the cake and cream, plus 15–30 minutes to decorate
Cooking time: 10-12 minutes for the cake
Oven temperature: moderately hot (200°C, 400°F, Gas Mark 6)

METRIC/IMPERIAL
For the chocolate roll:
1 teaspoon dried yeast
1 tablespoon lukewarm water
100 g/4 oz plain chocolate
75 g/3 oz butter
4 eggs
125 g/4½ oz sugar
125 g/4½ oz flour
For the chestnut cream:
125 g/4½ oz butter
300 g/11 oz chestnut purée
2 tablespoons kirsch
For the decoration:
100 g/4 oz plain chocolate

AMERICAN
For the chocolate roll:
1 teaspoon active dry yeast
1 tablespoon lukewarm water
4 squares semi-sweet chocolate
6 tablespoons butter
4 eggs
generous ½ cup sugar
1 cup plus 2 tablespoons flour
For the chestnut cream:
generous ½ cup butter
1⅓ cups chestnut purée
3 tablespoons kirsch
For the decoration:
4 squares semi-sweet chocolate

To make the chocolate roll Line a 24 × 34-cm/ 9½ × 13½-inch Swiss roll tin with greaseproof paper. Grease the lined tin.

Dissolve the yeast in the lukewarm water until frothy.

Melt the chocolate and butter together in a bowl over a saucepan of hot water.

Separate the eggs. In a large bowl, beat the egg yolks with the sugar until the mixture is pale and creamy. Add the yeast liquid and flour and then the melted chocolate and butter. Mix well.

Whisk the egg whites until stiff. Lightly fold them in. Pour the mixture into the prepared tin and spread out evenly.

Bake in a moderately hot oven for 10–12 minutes. Take care that the cake neither burns nor dries out.

Turn out on to a clean tea towel and remove the lining paper. With a sharp knife, trim the edges and make an indentation along one of the shorter edges to help with the rolling. Cover with a sheet of buttered greaseproof paper, buttered side to the cake. Roll up the cake using the tea towel as a guide. Allow to stand in the tea towel for a few minutes then place on a wire tray and leave to cool. When the cake is cool, unroll carefully and remove the paper. This roll is a little more fragile than normal.

To make the chestnut cream Beat the butter in a warm bowl until creamy. Stir in the chestnut purée and kirsch.

To assemble the cake Carefully spread about half the cream over the unrolled cake. Roll again carefully. The rest of the cream should be spread over the outside of the cake. Leave to stand in the refrigerator for several hours until very firm. Then cut off the two ends slantwise.

To decorate To decorate quickly, grate the chocolate roughly into curls with a potato peeler, pressing hard on the knife. Arrange these on the cake.

For a more painstaking presentation, prepare real chocolate caraque. Spread melted chocolate on a marble or laminated surface. Leave to cool until almost firm. Using a sharp knife, draw the knife blade towards you across the chocolate at a cutting angle to make thin rolls.

Serves 8-10

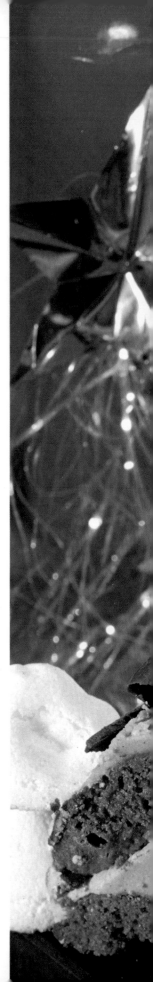

Saint-Émilion

**Preparation time: 15 minutes, plus 40 minutes to assemble and ice.
Prepare at least 12 hours in advance**

METRIC/IMPERIAL
150 g/5 oz butter, softened
150 g/5 oz icing sugar
1 egg yolk
6 tablespoons warmed milk
100 g/4 oz plain chocolate
1 tablespoon water
6 tablespoons brandy
500 g/1 lb 2 oz almond macaroons
  (or ratafias)
For the chocolate icing:
50 g/2 oz plain chocolate
2 tablespoons water
knob of butter

AMERICAN
$\frac{2}{3}$ cup softened butter
$1\frac{1}{4}$ cups confectioners' sugar
1 egg yolk
$\frac{1}{2}$ cup warmed milk
4 squares semi-sweet chocolate
1 tablespoon water
$\frac{1}{2}$ cup brandy
18 oz almond macaroons (or ratafias)

For the chocolate frosting:
2 squares semi-sweet chocolate
3 tablespoons water
nut of butter

Cream the softened butter and sugar together with a wooden spoon or electric mixer. The mixture should be very soft.

In a bowl, whisk the egg yolk and the warm milk together.

Finally melt the chocolate with 1 tablespoon water in a bowl over a saucepan of hot water. When melted remove from the heat and slowly add the milk and egg mixture, stirring continuously. Allow to cool. Pour this chocolate mixture into the creamed butter and sugar and beat for a few minutes until light and frothy.

Grease a 14-cm/5$\frac{1}{2}$-inch charlotte mould. Mix the water and brandy on a plate. Cover the base and sides of the mould with a layer of macaroons lightly dipped in this mixture, placing the flat sides to the mould.

Spoon in a good layer of chocolate cream. Cover with a layer of macaroons dipped in brandy.

Fill the mould in this way alternating layers of chocolate cream and macaroons dipped in brandy. Finish with a layer of macaroons placed flat side up.

Place a weight on a plate and cover the mould with it. Leave to stand in the refrigerator overnight.

Turn the cake out on to a serving dish and pour over the chocolate icing.

To make the chocolate icing Melt the chocolate with the water in a bowl over a saucepan of hot water. Add a knob of butter and allow to cool slightly. Pour over the top of the cake so that it trickles down the sides.

Serve chilled.

Serves 6–8

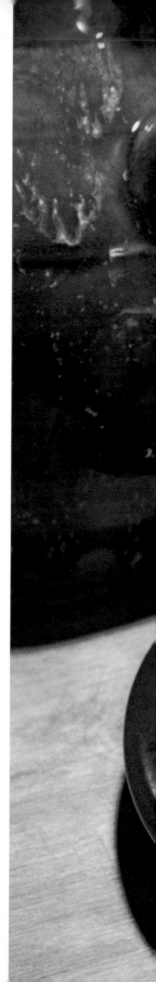

Brazilian charlotte

Preparation time: 30 minutes, plus 2 hours setting time for the ice cream and 2 hours for the charlotte

METRIC/IMPERIAL
For the filling:
125 g/5 oz icing sugar
300 ml/½ pint double cream
2–3 tablespoons coffee essence
For the charlotte:
150 ml/¼ pint very strong black coffee
2 sugar cubes
27 sponge fingers
For the decoration:
150 ml/¼ pint double cream, whipped
candied coffee beans

AMERICAN
For the filling:
1¼ cups confectioners' sugar
1¼ cups heavy cream
3–4 tablespoons coffee extract
For the charlotte:
⅔ cup very strong black coffee
2 sugar cubes
27 lady fingers
For the decoration:
⅔ cup whipped heavy cream
candied coffee beans

Add the sugar to the cream and whip until thick. Flavour with the coffee essence.

Pour the cream into an ice tray and place in the ice-making compartment of the refrigerator, turned to maximum coldness. Leave to freeze for about 2 hours when the cream will be firm enough.

Sweeten the coffee with the sugar lumps.

Line the base and sides of a 15–18 cm/ 6–7 inch charlotte mould with sponge fingers dipped in the sweet black coffee. In the centre place the iced cream. Cut off the sponge fingers level with the iced cream and cover the surface with these portions. Leave to set for a minimum of 2 hours.

To serve Turn out of the mould and decorate with freshly whipped cream and candied coffee beans.

Serves 6

Four flavour cream

Preparation time: 40 minutes
Cooking time: 5 minutes

METRIC/IMPERIAL
1 litre/1¾ pints milk
2 whole eggs
3 egg yolks
150 g/5 oz sugar
50 g/2 oz flour
50 g/2 oz butter
For the flavouring:
1 teaspoon coffee essence
1 tablespoon cocoa powder
1 tablespoon milk
few drops vanilla essence
40 g/1½ oz cube sugar
1–2 tablespoons water

AMERICAN
4¼ cups milk
2 whole eggs
3 egg yolks
⅔ cup sugar
½ cup flour
¼ cup butter
For the flavoring:
1 teaspoon coffee extract
1 tablespoon cocoa powder
1 tablespoon milk
few drops vanilla extract
1½ oz cube sugar
2–3 tablespoons water

Bring the milk to the boil.

Meanwhile, mix the eggs (2 whole and 3 yolks) with the sugar and flour. Into this mixture pour the boiling milk, stirring continuously, slowly at first, then more quickly.

Pour back into the saucepan and thicken, stirring vigorously until it begins to boil. Remove from the heat and add the butter. Pour the mixture into 4 bowls.

Flavour each one differently: the first with coffee essence (or powdered coffee), the second with cocoa (mixed to a cream with 1 tablespoon milk), the third with vanilla and the last with caramel, made with the cube sugar and water (illustrated recipe, page 38).

Stop the caramel cooking by diluting it with 3 tablespoons (u.s. ¼ cup) hot water. Use this thick liquid to flavour the cream.

Finally pour the four creams simultaneously into a large bowl (you will need two people holding a bowl in each hand). They will not mix, and will create a very pleasant appearance. Serve chilled.

Serves 8

NOTE Do not be put off by this unusual cream, for the only difficulty lies in the necessity of having two people to pour the four creams into the serving dish.

Grenoble coffee cake

Preparation time: 25 minutes, plus 10 minutes
Cooking time: 40-50 minutes
Oven temperature: moderately hot (190°C, 375°F, Gas Mark 5)

METRIC/IMPERIAL	AMERICAN
5 eggs, separated	5 eggs, separated
250 g/9 oz castor sugar	1 cup plus 2 tablespoons sugar
2 tablespoons rum	3 tablespoons rum
225 g/8 oz shelled walnuts, very finely chopped	2 cups very finely chopped walnuts
100 g/4 oz potato flour	scant cup potato starch
For the icing:	*For the frosting:*
150 g/5 oz icing sugar	1¼ cups confectioners' sugar
2 tablespoons coffee essence	3 tablespoons coffee extract
1–2 tablespoons water	about 2 tablespoons water
walnut halves for decoration	walnut halves for decoration

Beat the yolks and castor sugar together to give a pale, creamy mixture. Add the rum. Whisk the egg whites stiffly and fold in gently. Add the nuts and potato flour.

Line the base of a 25-cm/10-inch round cake tin with greaseproof paper. Grease the paper and pour the mixture into the tin. Bake in a moderately hot oven for 40–50 minutes.

Turn out of the tin on to a cooling tray.

While still warm add the coffee icing.

Sift the icing sugar into a bowl and into the centre pour 1 tablespoon coffee essence. Gradually add more coffee essence when the mixture becomes too thick. If the liquid is insufficient to make the icing run, add water in very small amounts (a few drops should be enough).

Pour the icing on to the centre of the cake, tilting the cake so that the whole surface is evenly coated.

Decorate with the walnuts.

Serves 8

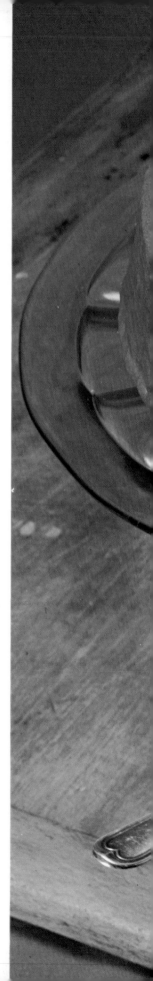

Carioca flan

Preparation time: 30 minutes
Cooking time: 10-15 minutes
Oven temperature: moderately hot (200°C, 400°F, Gas Mark 6)

METRIC/IMPERIAL
For the pastry:
50 g/2 oz butter
125 g/4½ oz flour
½ teaspoon salt
75 g/3 oz shelled walnuts, finely grated
50 g/2 oz castor sugar
1 egg yolk
2 tablespoons milk
For the filling:
2 eggs
100 g/4 oz sugar
200 ml/7 fl oz very strong black coffee
100 g/4 oz shelled walnuts, grated
1 tablespoon flour
walnut halves for decoration

AMERICAN
For the dough:
¼ cup butter
1 cup plus 2 tablespoons flour
½ teaspoon salt
¾ cup finely grated walnuts
¼ cup sugar
1 egg yolk
3 tablespoons milk
For the filling:
2 eggs
½ cup sugar
¾ cup very strong black coffee
1 cup grated walnuts
1 tablespoon flour
walnut halves for decoration

First prepare a nut flan pastry. In a bowl rub the butter into the flour, add the salt, grated nuts and sugar. Bind the pastry with the egg yolk, and milk if necessary, to give it a rolling consistency.

Roll the pastry to a thickness of 5 mm/¼ inch and line a lightly greased 20-cm/8-inch flan tin with it. Bake blind for 10 minutes.

Beat the eggs vigorously with a fork.

Heat the sugar and strong coffee until a froth forms. Pour this liquid while still very hot into the eggs, beating continuously, then stir this cream into the nuts and flour in a bowl. Return to the saucepan and stir over a low heat until the mixture thickens. Cool slightly.

Pour this mixture into the flan case and bake in a moderately hot oven for about 10–15 minutes.

Remove from the flan tin when cool and decorate with the walnuts.

Serves 6

Coffee vacherin

Preparation time: 20 minutes

METRIC/IMPERIAL
500 ml/17 fl oz coffee ice cream:
  see Brazilian Charlotte, page 120
1 (28-g/1-oz) sachet vanilla sugar
300 ml/½ pint double cream
50 g/2 oz icing sugar
1 egg white (optional)
250 g/9 oz small round meringues (petits
  fours size)
candied coffee beans for decoration

AMERICAN
1 pint coffee ice cream: see
  Brazilian Charlotte, page 120
1 (1-oz) envelope vanilla sugar
1¼ cups heavy cream
½ cup confectioners' sugar
1 egg white (optional)
9 oz small round meringues (petits
  fours size)
candied coffee beans for decoration

Prepare the coffee ice cream or buy it ready made.

Cover a cake plate with a paper doily and place in the refrigerator so that it will be very cold when you come to assemble the dessert.

Whip the vanilla sugar into the cream, add the sugar and, if preferred, to give a lighter consistency whip in a stiffly beaten egg white.

Place this cream in a sieve or a fine colander and stand over a bowl in the refrigerator for about 1 hour so that it will be firmer when you come to use it.

To assemble the dessert, arrange about half of the meringues over the base of the cold plate. Cover quickly with coffee ice cream.

Arrange the other meringues over the ice cream. Finally pipe rosettes of cream on top and decorate with candied coffee beans.

Serve at once.

Serves 8

Blackcurrant bavarois

Preparation time: 30 minutes. Make 24 hours in advance

METRIC/IMPERIAL
675 g/1½ lb blackcurrants
5 leaves gelatine or 15 g/½ oz powdered
 gelatine
250 g/9 oz sugar
6 tablespoons water
300 ml/½ pint double cream
50 g/2 oz icing sugar
For the decoration:
few sprigs blackcurrants
whipped cream

AMERICAN
1½ lb black currants
5 leaves gelatin or 2½ envelopes
 gelatin
1 cup plus 2 tablespoons sugar
½ cup water
1¼ cups heavy cream
½ cup confectioners' sugar
For the decoration:
few sprigs black currants
whipped cream

Liquidise the blackcurrants then sieve to remove any pips. This quantity of fruit gives about 450 ml/¾ pint (U.S. 2 cups) blackcurrant purée.

Soften the leaf gelatine in a bowl of cold water for 1 hour, or soften the powdered gelatine in 3 tablespoons (U.S. ¼ cup) cold water and stand the bowl over a pan of hot water to dissolve it.

Heat the sugar and water gently until the sugar has dissolved, then bring to the boil.

Remove from the heat. Add the black-currant purée and the dissolved powdered gelatine or the gelatine leaves which have been shaken to remove excess water. On contact with the hot liquid they will melt at once. Stir well during this operation. Then strain the mixture through a fine sieve to get rid of any bits of gelatine that failed to mix. Leave until quite cold.

Whip the cream and carefully fold into the cold mixture with the icing sugar.

Pour into a charlotte mould lined with greaseproof paper. Leave to stand for 24 hours in the refrigerator or until set.

To remove from the mould, stand the mould in hot water for 30 seconds. Wipe the mould and turn out on to a plate. Decorate with a few sprigs of black-currants and piped cream.

Serves 6

NOTE This dessert can be made with other fruits, such as strawberries or raspberries.

Redcurrant cream puffs

Preparation time: 25 minutes
Cooking time: 30–40 minutes
Oven temperature: moderately hot (200 °C, 400 °F, Gas Mark 6)

METRIC/IMPERIAL
225 g/8 oz redcurrants
For the choux pastry: illustrated recipe,
   page 35
75 g/3 oz butter
250 ml/8 fl oz water
½ teaspoon salt
1 tablespoon sugar
150 g/5 oz flour
4 medium-sized eggs
For the crème Chantilly:
   illustrated recipe, page 25
75 g/3 oz icing sugar
1 (28-g/1-oz) sachet vanilla sugar
300 ml/½ pint double cream
icing sugar to decorate

AMERICAN
½ lb red currants
For the choux paste: illustrated recipe,
   page 35
6 tablespoons butter
1 cup water
½ teaspoon salt
1 tablespoon sugar
1¼ cups flour
4 medium-sized eggs
For the crème Chantilly:
   illustrated recipe, page 25
scant ¾ cup confectioners' sugar
1 (1-oz) envelope vanilla sugar
1¼ cups heavy cream
confectioners' sugar to decorate

Wash and dry the redcurrants and remove the stalks.

Make the choux pastry (see page 35). Place tablespoons of the choux paste on a greased baking sheet, spacing out well as the choux will double in size during cooking.

Bake in a moderately hot oven for 30–40 minutes. Do not remove until completely cooked (check by feeling the weight of the choux puffs which should be firm and light). Leave to cool on a wire tray.

Make the crème Chantilly (see page 25). Gently stir in the prepared redcurrants.

With scissors cut the choux puffs two-thirds of the way through. Fill with the redcurrant cream and replace the lids.

Finally sprinkle with icing sugar through a fine sieve. These cream puffs should be eaten immediately.

The cream puffs can alternatively be filled with wild strawberries or raspberries.

Serves 6–8

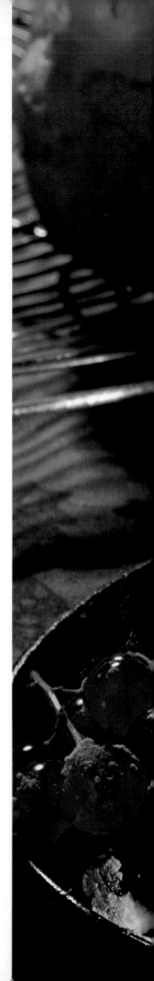

Currants in raspberry juice

Preparation time: 20 minutes

METRIC/IMPERIAL
450 g/1 lb red and white currants
225 g/8 oz raspberries
150 g/5 oz castor sugar

AMERICAN
1 lb red and white currants
½ lb raspberries
⅔ cup superfine sugar

Wash the currants and remove the stalks. Place in a dish.

Wash the raspberries. Place in a small saucepan. Heat gently, crushing the fruit with the back of a spoon. When boiling, filter the juice through a fine sieve, carefully squeezing the pulp and pips.

Add the sugar to the raspberry juice and pour the juice over the currants while still warm. Leave to stand in a cool place until serving.

Serve the fruit as they are or in individual goblets with whipped cream.

Serves 4-6

VARIATIONS
Strawberries in raspberry juice can be prepared in the same way. Decorate with slices of lemon.

Raspberry sauce can also be served with peaches or poached pears, or with vanilla ice cream.

Redcurrant pudding

Preparation time: 20 minutes
Cooking time: 40 minutes
Oven temperature: moderate (180°C, 350°F, Gas Mark 4)

METRIC/IMPERIAL
400 g/14 oz redcurrants
12 slices stale bread
500 ml/17 fl oz milk
1 vanilla pod, pierced
3 whole eggs
1 egg yolk
200 g/7 oz sugar

AMERICAN
14 oz red currants
12 slices stale bread
2 cups milk
1 vanilla bean, pierced
3 whole eggs
1 egg yolk
scant cup sugar

Wash the redcurrants and remove the stalks.

Generously grease an ovenproof dish. Remove the crusts from the bread, butter them and cut into triangles.

Sprinkle a few redcurrants in the bottom of the dish. Arrange some pieces of bread on top in a rosette shape. Continue with alternate layers of redcurrants and buttered bread.

Serves 6

NOTE Since the currant season is short, this recipe can be made with other seasonal fruits: bitter cherries, apricots or even plums. If using a very sweet fruit decrease the amount of sugar in the recipe.

Bring the milk to the boil with the vanilla pod. Beat the whole eggs plus the yolk well and beat in the sugar. Then gradually pour in the hot milk. Pour this custard over the bread and redcurrants. Leave to stand for at least 20 minutes so that the liquid soaks into the bread.

Bake in a moderate oven for 40 minutes until the pudding is well risen and brown.

When cooked, serve at once like a soufflé.

Dried fruit compote

Preparation time: 5 minutes. Make 1 day in advance
Cooking time: 50 minutes

METRIC/IMPERIAL
100 g/4 oz prunes
100 g/4 oz dried apricots
100 g/4 oz dried peaches
100 g/4 oz dried pears
1 litre/1¾ pints water
½ vanilla pod, pierced
150–200 g/5–7 oz sugar

AMERICAN
¼ lb prunes
¼ lb dried apricots
¼ lb dried peaches
¼ lb dried pears
4¼ cups water
½ vanilla bean, pierced
⅔–1 cup sugar

Carefully wash the fruits. Place in a bowl and cover with the water. Leave to soak for 12 hours.

Pour the fruit with the water into a saucepan, add the vanilla pod, cover and cook for 45 minutes. Then add the sugar and boil vigorously for 5 minutes.

Pour into a fruit bowl and leave to cool. Remove the vanilla pod and serve chilled.

Serves 6

Twelfth Night tart

Preparation time: 30 minutes
Cooking time: 15–20 minutes for the apricots, plus 50 minutes for the pie
Oven temperature: moderately hot (200°C, 400°F, Gas Mark 6) reducing
  to moderate (180°C, 350°F, Gas Mark 4)

METRIC/IMPERIAL	AMERICAN
For the fruit:	*For the fruit:*
225 g/8 oz dried apricots	½ lb dried apricots
500 ml/17 fl oz water	2 cups water
100 g/4 oz sugar	½ cup sugar
1 vanilla pod, pierced	1 vanilla bean, pierced
For the pastry:	*For the dough:*
400 g/14 oz flour	3½ cups flour
150 g/5 oz butter	⅔ cup butter
100 g/3½ oz sugar	½ cup sugar
grated rind of 1 lemon	grated rind of 1 lemon
good pinch of salt	good dash of salt
2 eggs, beaten	2 eggs, beaten

One day in advance soak the washed dried apricots in the water.

Cook the apricots over a low heat in the soaking water with the sugar and vanilla pod.

Meanwhile prepare the pastry. Place the flour, butter, sugar, grated lemon rind and salt in a mixing bowl and rub with the fingertips into a rough mixture.

Add the eggs and work into a dough. Knead the pastry, pressing down several times with the palm of the hand, and form into a ball.

Divide the pastry into 2 pieces and roll out to about 1 cm/½ inch thick.

Remove the vanilla pod and reduce the stewed apricots, together with the cooking water, to a purée.

Line a 23-cm/9-inch flan tin with half the pastry. Fill with the puréed apricots.

Top with the second half of the pastry, pressing the edges firmly together. Brush with beaten egg. Mark the swirls on top of the tart with a small knife. Bake in a moderately hot oven for 30 minutes, then reduce to moderate for 20 minutes longer. Cover with foil if becoming too brown.

Serves 8

NOTE The French often slip a trinket into the tart before cooking. Traditionally the guest who gets the slice with the trinket in it is supposed to have good luck throughout the year.

Epiphany tart

Preparation time: 15 minutes, plus extra time to make the pastry
Cooking time: 10–12 minutes
Oven temperature: hot (220°C, 425°F, Gas Mark 7)

METRIC/IMPERIAL
For the pâte feuilletée :
  illustrated recipe, page 29
200 g/7 oz flour
6 tablespoons water
½ teaspoon salt
150 g/5 oz butter
For the almond cream :
75 g/3 oz sugar
75 g/3 oz ground almonds
1 egg, beaten
1 tablespoon rum

AMERICAN
For the pâte feuilletée :
  illustrated recipe, page 29
1¾ cups flour
½ cup water
½ teaspoon salt
⅔ cup butter
For the almond cream :
6 tablespoons sugar
¾ cup ground almonds
1 egg, beaten
1 tablespoon rum

Make the pâte feuilletée (see page 29).

Place the sugar and ground almonds in a basin and mix in sufficient beaten egg until a stiff paste is formed. Stir in the rum.

Divide the pastry in two and roll each half into a 20-cm/8-inch circle. Place on a dampened baking sheet. On one circle mark out a design using a sharp knife and brush well with any remaining beaten egg. Bake the pastry circles in a hot oven for 10–12 minutes.

Allow to cool slightly then sandwich the cooked pastry circles together with the almond cream. Serve while still warm.

Serves 6

VARIATION
In place of the almond cream in the main recipe, this pie may be filled with marzipan cream:

1 whole egg, 1 egg yolk, 50 g/2 oz (U.S. ¼ cup) sugar, 25 g/1 oz (U.S. ¼ cup) flour, pinch of salt, 250 ml/8 fl oz (U.S. 1 cup) milk, 1 pierced vanilla pod (U.S. vanilla bean), 50 g/2 oz (U.S. ½ cup) almonds, 2 teaspoons orange flower water.

Mix together the whole egg, the egg yolk, sugar, flour and salt.

Boil the milk with the pierced vanilla pod.

Remove the vanilla pod and pour the hot milk gradually on to the mixture, stirring continuously. Pour the mixture into a saucepan.

Thicken over a low heat, stirring continuously with a wooden spoon; remove from the heat after the first bubble.

Blanch the almonds by dipping in a little water which has been brought to the boil. Remove the coloured skins.

Grate the almonds finely and place in a porcelain mortar. With the pestle crush the almonds, adding a few drops of orange blossom water from time to time.

When the almonds have the consistency of a smooth cream, stop pounding. Add this paste to the cream while still hot.

Sprinkle the surface of the cream with a little castor sugar to prevent a skin forming as it cools.

Hazelnut cake

Preparation time: 35 minutes
Cooking time: 50 minutes–1 hour
Oven temperature: moderately hot (190°C, 375°F, Gas Mark 5)

METRIC/IMPERIAL
100 g/4 oz hazelnuts, roughly chopped
6 egg whites
200 g/7 oz castor sugar
25 g/1 oz flour
100 g/4 oz butter, melted

AMERICAN
1 cup roughly chopped hazelnuts
6 egg whites
scant cup sugar
¼ cup flour
½ cup melted butter

Toast the chopped hazelnuts by placing them for a few minutes on a tray in a hot oven. Allow to cool.

Mix the unbeaten egg whites and sugar until smooth. Add the hazelnuts, then the sifted flour, and finally the melted butter.

Pour the mixture into a greased 20-cm/8-inch sandwich cake tin. Cook in a moderately hot oven for 50 minutes–1 hour.

Serves 6

VARIATION
Almond cake can be made in the same way replacing the hazelnuts with ground almonds. When cool, sprinkle the cake with icing sugar.

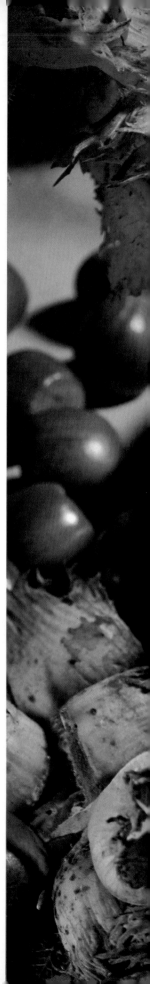

Prune flan

Preparation time: 35 minutes
Cooking time: 30-40 minutes
Oven temperature: moderately hot (200°C, 400°F, Gas Mark 6)

METRIC/IMPERIAL
For the pâte brisée: illustrated recipe,
  page 28
125 g/4½ oz flour
60 g/2¼ oz butter
pinch of salt
1 tablespoon sugar
1-2 tablespoons water
For the filling:
400 g/14 oz prunes
4 tablespoons apricot jam
4 tablespoons Cointreau
2 teaspoons demerara sugar

AMERICAN
For the pâte brisée: illustrated recipe,
  page 28
1 cup plus 2 tablespoons flour
4½ tablespoons butter
dash of salt
1 tablespoon sugar
2-3 tablespoons water
For the filling:
14 oz prunes
⅓ cup apricot jam
⅓ cup Cointreau
2 teaspoons raw cane sugar

Wash the prunes well and soak overnight.
  Make the pâte brisée (see page 28).
Form the pastry into a ball without
kneading and leave to stand for 1 hour.
  Drain and stone the prunes.
  Roll out the pastry to 3 mm/⅛ inch
thickness and line a lightly greased 18-cm/

7-inch flan tin. Fill the flan with the
prunes. Bake in a moderately hot oven
for 30-40 minutes.
  Remove the flan from the oven and while
still hot spread over the apricot jam dissolved in the Cointreau. Sprinkle with
demerara sugar. Serve hot or cold.

Serves 6

Light fruit cake

Preparation time: 25 minutes
Cooking time: about 1 hour
Oven temperature: moderately hot (200°C, 400°F, Gas Mark 6) reducing
  to moderate (180°C, 350°F, Gas Mark 4)

METRIC/IMPERIAL	AMERICAN
100 g/4 oz currants	$\frac{2}{3}$ cup currants
100 g/4 oz sultanas	$\frac{2}{3}$ cup seedless raisins
150 g/5 oz mixed glacé fruit	$\frac{3}{4}$ cup mixed candied fruit
3 tablespoons rum	$\frac{1}{4}$ cup rum
7 g/$\frac{1}{4}$ oz dried yeast	$\frac{1}{2}$ package active dry yeast
2 tablespoons warm water	3 tablespoons warm water
175 g/6 oz butter	$\frac{3}{4}$ cup butter
125 g/4$\frac{1}{2}$ oz castor sugar	generous $\frac{1}{2}$ cup sugar
3 eggs	3 eggs
225 g/8 oz flour	2 cups flour
$\frac{1}{2}$ teaspoon salt	$\frac{1}{2}$ teaspoon salt

Wash the currants and sultanas and cut the glacé fruit into pieces. Steep them together in the rum.

Mix the dried yeast in the warm water and stand in a warm place until frothy.

In a mixing bowl cut the butter into pieces and leave to soften in the warmth of the room. Add the sugar and cream until light and fluffy. Then beat in the eggs one at a time continuing to beat thoroughly between each egg. With the last egg the dough may appear to curdle: this does not matter.

Add the sifted flour with the yeast liquid and salt. Stir well so that the mixture becomes completely smooth.

Finally add the fruit and any rum that has not been absorbed, making sure that they are mixed in well.

Line a 1-kg/2-lb loaf tin with greaseproof paper and grease. Fill with the mixture, smoothing the surface evenly.

Bake in a moderately hot oven for 10 minutes, then lower to moderate for a further 40–50 minutes until risen and brown. Cover with foil if becoming too brown.

Turn out of the tin and leave to cool. Serve sliced, spread with butter.

Serves 8

NOTE A few glacé cherries may be placed on top of the loaf before baking, but care must be taken to prevent them browning.

Empress rice

Preparation time: 1 hour. Make 1 day in advance preferably
Cooking time: about 20-25 minutes for the rice

METRIC/IMPERIAL
2 gelatine leaves or 7 g/¼ oz powdered
  gelatine
100 g/4 oz glacé fruits
2 tablespoons kirsch
6 tablespoons double cream
For the rice pudding:
100 g/4 oz round-grain rice
500 ml/17 fl oz milk
50 g/2 oz sugar
For the custard:
  illustrated recipe, page 22
2 egg yolks
50 g/2 oz sugar
200 ml/7 fl oz milk
glacé fruits to decorate

AMERICAN
2 gelatin leaves or 1 envelope
  gelatin
½ cup candied fruits
3 tablespoons kirsch
½ cup heavy cream
For the rice pudding:
½ cup round-grain rice
2 cups milk
¼ cup sugar
For the custard:
  illustrated recipe, page 22
2 egg yolks
¼ cup sugar
1 cup milk
candied fruits to decorate

If using leaf gelatine, soften it in cold water to cover for about 1 hour.

Cook the rice pudding in the usual way. Wash the rice, cook in boiling water for 2 minutes and drain off the water. Finish cooking very slowly in boiling milk with the saucepan partially covered. Add the sugar at the end of the cooking, when all the milk is absorbed. The rice will then be tender and creamy. Leave to cool.

While the rice is cooking, cut the glacé fruits into small pieces and steep in the kirsch.

Prepare the custard (see page 22).

Add the softened gelatine to the hot custard. It will melt at once. Stir well and leave to cool. If using powdered gelatine, soften it in 2–3 tablespoons (U.S. ¼ cup) cold water and stand the bowl over a pan of hot water to dissolve it. Stir into the hot custard. Whisk the cream.

Mix together the rice and cold custard. Add the steeped glacé fruits then fold in the whipped cream.

Pour the mixture into a moistened fluted mould. Chill in the refrigerator until the following day.

To remove from the mould, stand the mould in hot water for 30 seconds. Wipe the mould and turn out on to the centre of a plate which has been in the refrigerator for 1 hour to become very cold. Decorate with glacé fruits.

This dish may be served with a sauce made by dissolving 225 g/8 oz redcurrant jelly in 3 tablespoons (U.S. ¼ cup) kirsch and 3 tablespoons (U.S. ¼ cup) water.

Serves 6-8

Old fashioned compote

Preparation time: 10 minutes
Cooking time: 20 minutes

METRIC/IMPERIAL
150 g/5 oz sugar
250 ml/8 fl oz wine
250 ml/8 fl oz water
pinch of cinnamon
4 pears
4 peaches
small bunch green grapes
small bunch black grapes

AMERICAN
$\frac{2}{3}$ cup sugar
1 cup wine
1 cup water
dash of cinnamon
4 pears
4 peaches
small bunch white grapes
small bunch purple grapes

Prepare a syrup by dissolving the sugar in the water, wine and cinnamon over a low heat.

Peel, quarter and core the pears. Peel the peaches, stone them and cut into quarters. Simmer the pears and peaches in the syrup until tender.

Drain the fruit and place in a serving dish.

Serves 6

Poach the grapes in the syrup for 1 minute only without allowing them to boil. Drain and mix with the other fruit.

Reduce the syrup by boiling rapidly until about 300 ml/$\frac{1}{2}$ pint (u.s. 1$\frac{1}{4}$ cups) remains. Pour over the fruit and serve chilled.

Grape flan

Preparation time: 30 minutes
Cooking time: 55 minutes
Oven temperature: moderately hot (200 °C, 400 °F, Gas Mark 6)

METRIC/IMPERIAL
For the pâte brisée: illustrated recipe,
  page 28
150 g/5 oz flour
75 g/2½ oz butter
pinch of salt
1 tablespoon castor sugar
2 tablespoons water
For the filling:
450 g/1 lb green grapes
2 eggs
3 tablespoons castor sugar
3 tablespoons ground almonds
3 tablespoons milk
3 tablespoons single cream
1 tablespoon kirsch

AMERICAN
For the pâte brisée: illustrated recipe,
  page 28
1¼ cups flour
5 tablespoons butter
dash of salt
1 tablespoon sugar
3 tablespoons water
For the filling:
1 lb white grapes
2 eggs
¼ cup sugar
¼ cup ground almonds
¼ cup milk
¼ cup light cream
1 tablespoon kirsch

Make the pâte brisée (see page 28) and
leave to stand for 30 minutes. Roll out and
line a 23-cm/9-inch flan tin, preferably
loose-bottomed. Bake blind in a moderately hot oven for 15 minutes.

Wash the grapes, pick off from the stalks
and dry thoroughly. Arrange evenly over
the pastry.

Beat the eggs with the sugar and ground
almonds. Gradually beat in the milk,
cream and kirsch.

Pour over the grapes and bake in a
moderately hot oven for 40 minutes.

Leave to cool before removing from the
tin.

Serves 6

NOTE This flan can also be made with
cherries or plums.

Lemon tart

Preparation time: 30 minutes
Cooking time: 45 minutes
Oven temperature: moderately hot (200°C, 400°F, Gas Mark 6)

METRIC/IMPERIAL
For the pâte brisée: illustrated recipe,
   page 28
200 g/7 oz flour
100 g/3½ oz butter
½ teaspoon salt
1 tablespoon sugar
3 tablespoons water
For the filling:
2 eggs
200 g/7 oz castor sugar
75 g/3 oz butter, melted
2 lemons

AMERICAN
For the pâte brisée: illustrated recipe,
   page 28
1¾ cups flour
scant ½ cup butter
½ teaspoon salt
1 tablespoon sugar
¼ cup water
For the filling:
2 eggs
scant cup sugar
6 tablespoons melted butter
2 lemons

Prepare the pâte brisée (see page 28) and leave to stand in a cool place for 30 minutes. Then roll out on a floured board and line a greased 24-cm/9½-inch square, loose-bottomed shallow tin or a 26-cm/10-inch round flan tin. Bake blind for 15 minutes.

Beat the eggs with the sugar until pale and creamy. Stir in the melted butter, the juice of 2 lemons and grated peel of 1 lemon.

Pour this cream into the pastry case and bake in a moderately hot oven for 30 minutes. The lemon filling will brown quickly and the tart should be covered with a piece of foil after 10–15 minutes.

Lift out of the tin while hot and leave to cool.

Serves 6

Lemon mousse

Preparation time: 20 minutes
Cooking time: 8–10 minutes

METRIC/IMPERIAL
3 eggs, separated
150 g/5 oz sugar
25 g/1 oz cornflour
200 ml/7 fl oz water
2 good lemons
25 g/1 oz butter

AMERICAN
3 eggs, separated
1¼ cups sugar
¼ cup cornstarch
¾ cup water
2 good lemons
2 tablespoons butter

Put the egg yolks in a small stainless steel saucepan with the sugar and mix together. Add the cornflour, then gradually stir in the water to give a smooth mixture.

Wash 1 of the lemons and finely grate the rind. Squeeze the juice from both lemons and add together with the grated rind to the mixture in the saucepan.

Thicken over a low heat stirring continu-ously until nearly boiling, but do not allow to boil. Remove from the heat and stir in the butter. Leave to cool.

Whisk the egg whites until stiff then fold very gently into the cream. Pour into small individual dishes.

Chill before serving and eat the same day.

Serves 5–6

Iced melon

Preparation time: 15 minutes

METRIC/IMPERIAL
150 g/5 oz sugar
6 tablespoons water
1 vanilla pod, pierced
3 Ogen melons
1 litre/1¾ pints vanilla ice cream

AMERICAN
⅔ cup sugar
½ cup water
1 vanilla bean, pierced
3 Cantaloupe melons
1 quart vanilla ice cream

Prepare the vanilla syrup. Bring the sugar and water to the boil with the pierced vanilla pod. Boil for 5 minutes then leave to cool. Remove the vanilla pod from the syrup.

Cut the melons in half. Remove the seeds and scoop the flesh out with a melon baller. Remove any remaining flesh from the skins. Place the melon balls in a bowl and pour over the vanilla syrup. Chill the melon balls and the empty skins.

Just before serving fill the melon skins with balls of vanilla ice cream mixed with the melon balls.

Place each half melon on a fruit dish to serve.

You can make your own vanilla ice cream by freezing a custard to which double cream has been added in the proportion of 150 ml/¼ pint (U.S. ⅔ cup) of cream to 1 litre/1¾ pints (U.S. 4¼ cups) of custard.

Serves 6

Melon surprise

Preparation time: 30 minutes. Make 3 or 4 hours in advance

METRIC/IMPERIAL
6 Ogen melons, the size of large
  oranges
225 g/8 oz wild strawberries or small
  strawberries
100 g/4 oz sugar
4 tablespoons orange liqueur

AMERICAN
6 Cantaloupe melons, the size of large
  oranges
½ lb wild strawberries or small
  strawberries
½ cup sugar
⅓ cup orange liqueur

Cut a lid off each melon at the stalk end (see photograph). Remove the flesh from inside the melons with a melon baller. Scoop out any remaining flesh.

Wash and hull the strawberries. Steep the melon balls and strawberries in the sugar and liqueur for several hours in a cool place.

To serve Fill the melon skins with the fruit salad, replace the lids and chill.

If strawberries are not available, you can serve the melon balls soaked in a muscadet and sprinkled with sugar. Chill for 2 hours before serving.

Serves 6

Ali-baba

Preparation time: 20 minutes, plus a minimum of 2½ hours standing time
Cooking time: 20–25 minutes
Oven temperature: hot (220°C, 425°F, Gas Mark 7)

METRIC/IMPERIAL

For the baba : illustrated recipe,
  page 37
150 g/5 oz flour
½ teaspoon salt
1 teaspoon sugar
2 eggs, beaten
15 g/½ oz dried yeast
3 tablespoons lukewarm milk
75 g/3 oz butter, melted
For the filling :
8 oranges
6 tablespoons weak tea
200 g/7 oz sugar
4 tablespoons kirsch
3 tablespoons water

AMERICAN

For the baba : illustrated recipe,
  page 37
1¼ cups flour
½ teaspoon salt
1 teaspoon sugar
2 eggs, beaten
1 package active dry yeast
¼ cup lukewarm milk
6 tablespoons melted butter
For the filling :
8 oranges
½ cup weak tea
scant cup sugar
⅓ cup kirsch
¼ cup water

Make the baba dough (see page 37) and place in a greased and floured 18-cm/7-inch ring mould. The tin should not be more than one-third full. Leave to stand again in a warm place for about 30 minutes until the dough is about 1 cm/½ inch below the top of the mould. Bake in a hot oven for 20–25 minutes until golden brown.

Squeeze the juice of 3 oranges, add the same volume of weak tea, half the sugar and half the kirsch. Heat gently until the

sugar has dissolved then bring to the boil.

Peel the remaining oranges, segment them and remove the pips. Steep in a syrup prepared from the water and remaining sugar and kirsch.

Turn the baba out of the mould on to a serving dish (one which is heatproof and quite shallow). While it is still hot pour over the hot syrup. Leave it to soak completely into the cake.

Fill the centre of the baba with the orange segments.

Serves 6

Orange and almond cake

Preparation time: 20 minutes
Cooking time: 50 minutes
Oven temperature: moderate (180°C, 350°F, Gas Mark 4)

METRIC/IMPERIAL	AMERICAN
4 eggs	4 eggs
100 g/4 oz castor sugar	½ cup sugar
100 g/4 oz ground almonds	1 cup ground almonds
2 juicy oranges	2 juicy oranges
2 tablespoons orange jelly	3 tablespoons orange jelly
50 g/2 oz toasted chopped almonds	½ cup toasted chopped almonds

Separate the eggs. Mix the yolks and the sugar together and beat until the mixture is pale and creamy.

Stir in the ground almonds, the grated rind of half an orange and the juice of both oranges. Finally whisk the egg whites until stiff and fold into the mixture.

Grease a 24-cm/9½-inch cake tin and line the base with well-greased grease-proof paper. This cake can be quite difficult to remove from the tin.

Pour the mixture into the cake tin and bake in a moderate oven for 50 minutes.

Before serving brush the cake with a little orange jelly and press toasted chopped almonds around the sides.

Serves 8

VARIATION
This cake can be flavoured with lemon instead of orange. Replace the orange jelly and toasted almonds with an icing prepared by dissolving 4 tablespoons (u.s. ⅓ cup) icing sugar with just enough lemon juice to give a thick, shiny cream, which is just runny. Pour the icing on to the centre of the cake and spread with a wide bladed knife. Leave to set.

Golden pancakes

Preparation time: 15 minutes, plus 1 hour standing time
Cooking time: 10 minutes for the filling; 20 minutes for the pancakes

METRIC/IMPERIAL
For the batter:
250 ml/8 fl oz milk
3 tablespoons water
125 g/4½ oz flour
2 eggs, separated
50 g/2 oz sugar
50 g/2 oz butter, melted
grated rind of ½ orange
½ teaspoon salt
For the filling:
1 orange
3 eggs
200 g/7 oz sugar
50 g/2 oz butter, melted
2 tablespoons orange liqueur

AMERICAN
For the batter:
1 cup milk
¼ cup water
1 cup plus 2 tablespoons flour
2 eggs, separated
¼ cup sugar
¼ cup melted butter
grated rind of ½ orange
½ teaspoon salt
For the filling:
1 orange
3 eggs
scant cup sugar
¼ cup melted butter
3 tablespoons orange liqueur

Heat the milk and water until just warm. Whisk in the flour and leave to stand for 1 hour.

After standing, stir in the beaten egg yolks, sugar, melted butter, grated orange rind and salt. Whisk the egg whites until softly whipped but not too stiff. Add to the batter and beat vigorously (preferably with a mixer) to give a perfectly uniform batter.

Grease a frying pan and heat. Pour in some of the batter, tilting the pan in all directions so that the entire base is covered. Cook each pancake over a moderate heat, and turn with a palette knife. The pancakes should be extremely thin: if the batter is too thick, add a little water.

While the batter is standing, prepare the filling. Wash the orange well, grate half the rind, then squeeze the juice.

Whisk together the eggs, sugar, orange juice and grated rind. Heat the mixture in a bowl over a saucepan of boiling water until it thickens a little and resembles honey. Remove from the heat before it boils. Stir in the butter and liqueur.

Spread a little of the filling on to each pancake and fold in four.

Eat hot or cold.

To keep hot, cover the serving dish with a sheet of foil. Seal well and place in a cool oven.

Makes about 15 pancakes

Orange fondant cake

Preparation time: 20 minutes
Cooking time: 30–40 minutes
Oven temperature: moderately hot (190°C, 375°F, Gas Mark 5)

METRIC/IMPERIAL	AMERICAN
100 g/4 oz butter	$\frac{1}{2}$ cup butter
100 g/4 oz sugar	$\frac{1}{2}$ cup sugar
2 eggs	2 eggs
1 large orange	1 large orange
1 teaspoon dried yeast	1 teaspoon active dry yeast
100 g/4 oz flour	1 cup flour
For the icing :	*For the frosting :*
150 g/5 oz icing sugar	$1\frac{1}{4}$ cups confectioners' sugar
1 large very juicy orange	1 large very juicy orange

Cream the butter with the sugar in a warm bowl. Add the eggs one at a time, continuing to beat the mixture well.

Grate the rind of the orange and squeeze the juice. Warm the juice until just at blood heat. Dissolve the yeast in the lukewarm orange juice and add to the creamed mixture. Fold in the flour and finely grated orange rind.

Grease and line the base of an 18-cm/7-inch square cake tin. Pour the mixture into the prepared tin and bake in a moderately hot oven for 30–40 minutes.

Meanwhile dissolve the icing sugar in the juice of the other orange to give a thick, runny icing. It may not be necessary to use all the orange juice.

When cooked, turn the cake out of the tin on to a plate and while still hot cover with half the icing. The cake should become soft.

Cover with the rest of the icing when the cake is completely cool. Decorate, if liked, with a slice of orange.

Serves 6

NOTE This cake is ideal for a buffet, in which case cut it into cubes when cool and place them in small paper cases. The cake will keep very well for 2 or 3 days in an airtight tin or covered in the refrigerator.

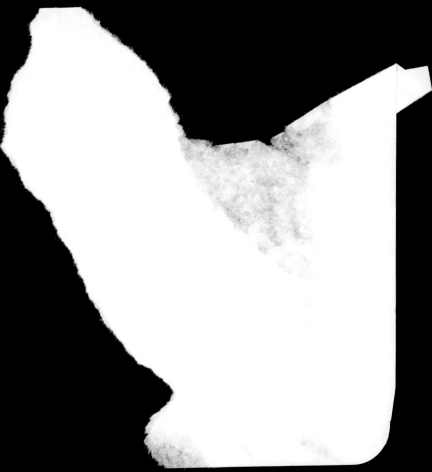

Snow cake

Preparation time: 25 minutes
Cooking time: 45 minutes
Oven temperature: moderately hot (190°C, 375°F, Gas Mark 5)

METRIC/IMPERIAL
7 egg whites
1 orange
250 g/9 oz castor sugar
50 g/2 oz flour, sifted
75 g/3 oz potato flour
100 g/4 oz butter, melted
For the decoration:
150 g/5 oz sugar
200 ml/7 fl oz water
2 tablespoons apricot jam
2 tablespoons rum

AMERICAN
7 egg whites
1 orange
1 cup plus 2 tablespoons sugar
½ cup sifted flour
scant ¾ cup potato starch
½ cup melted butter
For the decoration:
⅔ cup sugar
1 cup water
3 tablespoons apricot jam
3 tablespoons rum

Whisk the egg whites until very stiff. Grate the rind of the orange and very gently fold into the egg whites with the sugar, flour, potato flour and melted butter. Keep the orange for the decoration.

Pour the mixture into a greased and floured 20-cm/8-inch cake tin and bake in a moderately hot oven for 45 minutes.

While the cake is baking prepare the decoration. Peel the pith off the orange, cut into rounds and remove the pips. Dissolve the sugar in the water over a low heat and poach the orange slices in this syrup until lightly caramelised.

When cooked, turn the cake out of the tin, decorate with the poached orange slices and top with the apricot jam mixed with the rum.

Serve cold.

Serves 6

VARIATION
Snow cake can also be flavoured with lemon rind and decorated with icing sugar.

Norwegian oranges

Preparation time: 40 minutes
Freezing time: 2–3 hours in the ice-making compartment of the
  refrigerator at the coldest setting
Cooking time: 3–5 minutes
Oven temperature: hot (230°C, 450°F, Gas Mark 8)

METRIC/IMPERIAL	AMERICAN
4 large juicy oranges	4 large juicy oranges
200 g/7 oz castor sugar	scant cup sugar
6 egg yolks	6 egg yolks
250 ml/8 fl oz double cream	1 cup heavy cream
For the meringue:	*For the meringue:*
4 egg whites	4 egg whites
200 g/7 oz icing sugar	1½ cups confectioners' sugar

Choose large, best quality, juicy oranges.

With a potato peeler remove the peel of one orange in a long strip. Halve the oranges and squeeze the juice, taking great care not to damage 6 of the skins, which will be used to serve the ice cream.

Place the orange juice, strip of peel and sugar in a stainless steel saucepan. Dissolve the sugar over a low heat then bring to the boil. Remove the orange peel.

Whisk the egg yolks with a fork while slowly pouring in the hot, sweetened orange juice. Pour back into the saucepan and thicken over a low heat, stirring continuously. Do not allow the mixture to boil.

Leave to cool completely. Whip the cream, fold into the mixture and freeze in an ice cream maker. If you do not have one, freeze in a suitable container and whisk 2 or 3 times during the freezing process. When the ice cream is frozen, fill the empty orange shells and place in the ice-making compartment of the refrigerator for 2–3 hours.

Prepare a cooked meringue in advance. Place the egg whites in a basin. Over a saucepan of hot, not boiling water add the icing sugar and beat, preferably with an electric mixer, until a firm, smooth meringue is formed.

A few minutes before the dessert is to be served, preheat the oven.

Place the half oranges containing the ice cream in an ovenproof dish (arranging them on a round of crumpled foil will make them more stable). Place ice cubes between the orange halves.

Pipe the meringue over the ice cream to completely cover it.

Place in the hot oven for 3–5 minutes, until the meringue is lightly browned.

Remove at once from the oven, arrange on a dish and serve immediately.

Serves 6

Orange soufflés

Preparation time: 45 minutes
Cooking time: 10–20 minutes
Oven temperature: hot (220°C, 425°F, Gas Mark 7)

METRIC/IMPERIAL	AMERICAN
6 large thick-skinned oranges	6 large thick-skinned oranges
3 eggs, separated	3 eggs, separated
100 g/4 oz castor sugar	½ cup sugar
2 tablespoons cornflour	3 tablespoons cornstarch
1 tablespoon orange liqueur	1 tablespoon orange liqueur

With a sharp knife cut the top from each orange. Also cut a thin round from the base so that the oranges stand upright.

Using a grapefruit knife or a teaspoon, gently remove the flesh from the oranges without damaging the skins.

Squeeze the flesh to obtain the juice, and strain it.

Beat together the egg yolks, sugar and cornflour. Dilute with the orange juice. Place over a low heat, stirring continuously. Remove from the heat when it begins to boil and the mixture has thickened.

Then add the orange liqueur. This mixture can be left to stand for some time.

About 30 minutes before serving the orange soufflés, whisk the egg whites stiffly and slowly fold into the orange cream. Fill the orange shells with this mixture.

Place in an ovenproof dish and bake in a hot oven for 10–20 minutes.

Serve immediately.

Serves 6

Andalouse flan

Preparation time: 1 hour
Cooking time: 25–30 minutes
Oven temperature: moderately hot (200°C, 400°F, Gas Mark 6)

METRIC/IMPERIAL

For the pastry:
1 egg yolk
50 g/2 oz castor sugar
125 g/4½ oz flour
50 g/2 oz butter
2 tablespoons water
1 teaspoon grated orange rind
For the apple purée:
  see Apple Charlotte, page 52
450 g/1 lb apples
75 g/3 oz castor sugar
1–2 tablespoons water
For the filling:
2 oranges
For the glaze:
3 tablespoons apricot jam, sieved
juice of ½ lemon

AMERICAN

For the dough:
1 egg yolk
¼ cup sugar
1 cup plus 2 tablespoons flour
¼ cup butter
3 tablespoons water
1 teaspoon grated orange rind
For the apple purée:
  see Apple Charlotte, page 52
1 lb apples
6 tablespoons sugar
2–3 tablespoons water
For the filling:
2 oranges
For the glaze:
¼ cup sieved apricot jam
juice of ½ lemon

Place the egg yolk, sugar, flour and butter in a mixing bowl. Rub in using the fingertips until the pastry has the appearance of coarse sand.

Add the water and grated orange rind. Knead until smooth then leave to stand for 30 minutes.

Meanwhile prepare a thick apple purée (see page 52).

Roll the pastry to a thickness of 3 mm/⅛ inch and line a 23-cm/9-inch flan tin.

Bake blind in a moderately hot oven for 10 minutes. Fill the half cooked pastry case with the apple purée and finish baking until the flan and apple are golden brown, about 15–20 minutes.

Leave until just warm. Peel the oranges close to the flesh, slice thinly and arrange over the flan.

Boil the apricot jam with the lemon juice for 2 minutes. Spread over the flan.

Serves 6

Peach melba

Preparation time: 20 minutes
Cooking time: 10 minutes

METRIC/IMPERIAL
3 large or 6 small peaches
200 g/7 oz sugar
6 tablespoons water
1 tablespoon kirsch
100 g/4 oz raspberries
1 (483-g/17-fl oz) block vanilla ice cream
25 g/1 oz flaked almonds, toasted

AMERICAN
3 large or 6 small peaches
scant cup sugar
½ cup water
1 tablespoon kirsch
¼ lb raspberries
1 pint vanilla ice cream
¼ cup toasted flaked almonds

Put the peaches into a bowl of boiling water, leave for ½ minute, then lift out and remove the skins. Cut in two and remove the stones. Dissolve half the sugar in the water over a low heat, then bring to the boil and cook for 2 minutes. Add the kirsch. Poach the peach halves for 5 minutes in this syrup. Leave to cool before draining.

Wash and crush the raspberries and cook for 5 minutes with the remaining sugar. Sieve and leave to cool also.

Assemble the melba in individual fruit dishes. Place in each some vanilla ice cream and 1 or 2 peach halves. Pour over raspberry purée and decorate with a few almonds.

Serves 6

VARIATION
Strawberry melba can be made in the same way. Use the strawberries uncooked, topped with raspberry or strawberry syrup and decorated with crème Chantilly (illustrated recipe, page 25) instead of the almonds.

Peach cream meringue

Preparation time: 20 minutes
Cooking time: 10 minutes for the crème pâtissière; 10 minutes for the fruit; 10 minutes for the meringue
Oven temperature: moderately hot (200°C, 400°F, Gas Mark 6)

METRIC/IMPERIAL
For the crème pâtissière:
 illustrated recipe, page 23
2 whole eggs
4 egg yolks
150 g/5 oz sugar
125 g/4½ oz flour
1 litre/1¾ pints milk
1 vanilla pod, pierced
50 g/2 oz butter
For the poached peaches:
1 kg/2 lb peaches
100 g/4 oz sugar
1 tablespoon kirsch
For the meringue:
4 egg whites
100 g/4 oz sugar
50 g/2 oz blanched almonds (optional)

AMERICAN
For the crème pâtissière:
 illustrated recipe, page 23
2 whole eggs
4 egg yolks
⅔ cup sugar
1 cup plus 2 tablespoons flour
4¼ cups milk
1 vanilla bean, pierced
¼ cup butter
For the poached peaches:
2 lb peaches
½ cup sugar
1 tablespoon kirsch
For the meringue:
4 egg whites
½ cup sugar
½ cup blanched almonds (optional)

Make the crème pâtissière (see page 23). Pour into an ovenproof dish.

Put the peaches into a bowl of boiling water, leave for ½ minute, then lift out and remove the skins. Cut in two and remove the stones. Poach gently with the sugar for 10 minutes over a low heat. Lightly flavour with kirsch.

Arrange the cooked peaches over the crème pâtissière.

Stiffly whisk the egg whites. Fold in the sugar and blanched almonds (if you wish to include them).

Cover the peaches completely with this meringue. Cook in a moderately hot oven for 10 minutes to brown the meringue, then remove from the oven and leave to cool. Place in the refrigerator.

This dish should be served chilled.

Serves 8-10

Peaches in port

Preparation time: 20 minutes

METRIC/IMPERIAL
150 g/5 oz castor sugar
6 tablespoons water
½ bottle dessert wine (port, muscat or
  malaga)
1 kg/2 lb peaches

AMERICAN
⅔ cup sugar
½ cup water
½ bottle dessert wine (port, muscat or
  malaga)
2 lb peaches

Dissolve the sugar in the water over a low heat, then bring to the boil and cook for 1 minute. Leave to cool then add the wine.

Put the peaches into a bowl of boiling water, leave for ½ minute, then lift out and remove the skins. Stone and quarter them.

Steep the pieces in the wine syrup. Leave to stand for at least 1 hour in the refrigerator before serving.

Serves 6–8

NOTE Out of season, use canned peaches. If liked, sprinkle with a few blanched almonds or mix in other fruits: 150 g/5 oz raspberries, for example.

Peaches Saint-Grégoire

Preparation time: 20 minutes
Cooking time: 10 minutes

METRIC/IMPERIAL
6 large peaches
200 g/7 oz sugar
500 ml/17 fl oz water
1 vanilla pod, pierced
1 round crustless loaf
75 g/3 oz butter
3 tablespoons redcurrant jelly

AMERICAN
6 large peaches
scant cup sugar
2 cups water
1 vanilla bean, pierced
1 round crustless loaf
6 tablespoons butter
¼ cup red currant jelly

Put the peaches into a bowl of boiling water, leave for ½ minute, then lift out and remove the skins. Halve the peaches and remove the stones. Dissolve the sugar in the water with the vanilla pod over a low heat. Then bring to the boil and cook for 3–4 minutes. Poach the peach halves in this syrup for about 10 minutes.

Avoid putting the fruit on top of each other in the saucepan. It is better to poach them in several batches.

Drain and leave to cool.

Cut 12 slices of crustless bread. Melt the butter in a frying pan and lightly fry the bread slices on both sides. Arrange on a dish.

Place half a peach on each slice of bread. Top with redcurrant jelly, warmed and diluted with a little of the poaching syrup.

In season decorate with sprigs of fresh redcurrants.

Serves 6

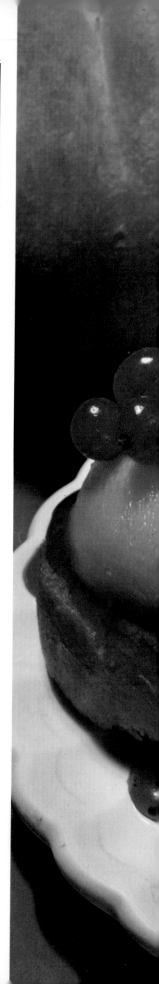

Pear cake

Preparation time: 30 minutes
Cooking time: 1–1¼ hours
Oven temperature: moderately hot (190°C, 375°F, Gas Mark 5)

METRIC/IMPERIAL	AMERICAN
4 pears	4 pears
lemon juice	lemon juice
15 g/½ oz dried yeast	1 package active dry yeast
2 tablespoons warm water	3 tablespoons warm water
4 eggs	4 eggs
250 g/9 oz castor sugar	1 cup plus 2 tablespoons sugar
125 g/4½ oz butter	generous ½ cup butter
250 g/9 oz flour	2¼ cups flour
½ teaspoon ground cinnamon	½ teaspoon ground cinnamon
¼ teaspoon vanilla essence	½ teaspoon vanilla extract
castor sugar to sprinkle	sugar to sprinkle

Peel the pears, halve and core them. Toss in a little lemon juice to prevent discoloration.

Blend the yeast with the water and leave in a warm place until frothy. Place the eggs in a basin with the sugar. Whisk or beat with a fork until the mixture becomes smooth and frothy. Soften the butter, then beat in a little at a time until well mixed. Stir in the flour, the yeast liquid, cinnamon and vanilla essence.

Grease a 20-cm/8-inch cake tin. Pour in the mixture and lay the pear halves on it, rounded sides uppermost. Sprinkle with castor sugar.

Cook in a moderately hot oven for 1–1¼ hours. Cover with foil if the cake browns too quickly. Leave to cool before turning out of the tin.

Serves 8–10

Russian pear custard

Preparation time: 45 minutes. Chill overnight

METRIC/IMPERIAL
2 gelatine leaves or 7 g/¼ oz powdered
  gelatine
450 g/1 lb ripe pears
100 g/4 oz sugar
1 liqueur glass kirsch
300 ml/½ pint double cream
For the custard:
  illustrated recipe, page 22
4 egg yolks
100 g/4 oz sugar
250 ml/8 fl oz milk
½ vanilla pod, pierced
For the caramel:
  illustrated recipe, page 38
50 g/2 oz cube sugar
2 tablespoons water

AMERICAN
2 gelatin leaves or 1 envelope
  gelatin
1 lb ripe pears
½ cup sugar
1 liqueur glass kirsch
1¼ cups heavy cream
For the custard:
  illustrated recipe, page 22
4 egg yolks
½ cup sugar
1 cup milk
½ vanilla bean, pierced
For the caramel:
  illustrated recipe, page 38
2 oz cube sugar
3 tablespoons water

Soften the leaf gelatine in a bowl of cold water for 1 hour. If using powdered gelatine, soften it in 2 tablespoons (U.S. 3 tablespoons) cold water and stand the bowl over a pan of hot water to dissolve it.

Prepare a thick, vanilla custard (see page 22).

Add the gelatine to the custard. Stir well to dissolve it and strain through a fine sieve. Leave until completely cold.

Make a caramel (see page 38) and coat the base and sides of a fluted tin or charlotte mould with the caramel.

When the custard is cold, peel the pears and remove the cores and pips. Reduce the pears to a purée in a liquidiser. This should be done very quickly for they soon turn brown.

Immediately add this purée of uncooked pears to the custard with the sugar and kirsch. Whisk the cream until softly whipped and fold into the custard.

Pour into the caramel-coated mould. Place in the refrigerator and chill overnight.

Turn out of the mould immediately before serving.

Serves 6

Pear tart du Berry

Preparation time: 20 minutes, plus 15 minutes
Cooking time: 1 hour
Oven temperature: moderately hot (190°C, 375°F, Gas Mark 5)

METRIC/IMPERIAL
For the pâte brisée:
  illustrated recipe, page 28
250 g/9 oz flour
125 g/4½ oz butter
½ teaspoon salt
2 tablespoons sugar
3 tablespoons water
For the filling:
675 g/1½ lb pears
3 tablespoons brandy
50 g/2 oz sugar
pinch of pepper
1 egg yolk to glaze
6 tablespoons double cream

AMERICAN
For the pâte brisée:
  illustrated recipe, page 28
2¼ cups flour
generous ½ cup butter
½ teaspoon salt
3 tablespoons sugar
¼ cup water
For the filling:
1½ lb pears
¼ cup brandy
¼ cup sugar
dash of pepper
1 egg yolk to glaze
½ cup heavy cream

Peel the pears, cut into thick slices and steep in the brandy, to which has been added the sugar and pepper, for 30 minutes.

Make the pâte brisée (see page 28) and leave to stand for 30 minutes. Roll out two-thirds of the pastry to a thickness of 3 mm/⅛ inch.

Line a 20-cm/8-inch porcelain or oven-proof glass flan dish as it is best to serve this tart in the baking dish. Trim the pastry to the edges of the dish.

Drain off the liquid from the pears and reserve. Arrange the pears in the pastry case.

Serves 6-8

NOTE Quince tart may also be prepared in the same way.

Roll the remaining pastry into a circle and cover the pears. Seal the edges with a little water. Cut out a round of pastry in the centre to allow the steam to escape during cooking.

Brush with egg yolk and bake in a moderately hot oven for 1 hour. Cover with foil after 40 minutes if browning too quickly.

When the tart is cooked and browned, mix the cream with the reserved liquor and pour through the central hole into the tart.

Serve hot preferably.

Agen pears

Preparation time: 15 minutes
Cooking time: 20-30 minutes

METRIC/IMPERIAL
For the prunes:
225 g/8 oz prunes
250 ml/8 fl oz water
250 ml/8 fl oz red Bordeaux wine
1 tablespoon sugar
For the pears:
450 g/1 lb small pears
100 g/4 oz sugar
1 (28-g/1-oz) sachet vanilla sugar
3 tablespoons water
juice of ½ lemon

AMERICAN
For the prunes:
½ lb prunes
1 cup water
1 cup red Bordeaux wine
1 tablespoon sugar
For the pears:
1 lb small pears
½ cup sugar
1 (1-oz) envelope vanilla sugar
¼ cup water
juice of ½ lemon

Soak the prunes overnight in the water and wine.

Add 1 tablespoon sugar and cook the prunes for a few minutes.

Peel, halve and core the pears. Dissolve the sugar and vanilla sugar in the water and lemon juice over a low heat. When the syrup begins to boil, add the prepared pears.

Cook gently until the fruit is soft, turning the pears frequently in the syrup. The cooking time will vary with the variety and ripeness of the fruit. Leave to cool.

Mix the fruits together and serve chilled.

Serves 6

Pears Hélène

Preparation time: 25 minutes

METRIC/IMPERIAL
1 (882-g/1 lb 13-oz) can pear halves
125 g/4½ oz plain chocolate
6 tablespoons water
5 sugar cubes
1 litre/1¾ pints vanilla ice cream

AMERICAN
1 (29-oz) can pear halves
4½ squares semi-sweet chocolate
½ cup water
5 sugar cubes
1 quart vanilla ice cream

Several hours before serving Drain the canned pears and leave to chill in the refrigerator.

Ten minutes before serving Break the chocolate into pieces and place with the water in a basin over a saucepan of hot water. Melt slowly, stirring until the sauce is smooth. Add the sugar cubes and cook slowly until the sugar has dissolved.

Just before serving Place the ice cream on a serving dish and mould into a smooth shape. Arrange the chilled pear halves around it.

Pour the hot chocolate sauce into a small jug and serve separately.

Serves 6

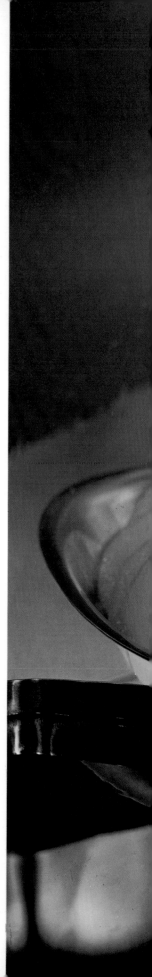

Chocolate pears

Preparation time: 20 minutes
Cooking time: 20–30 minutes (according to the variety and ripeness of the fruit)

METRIC/IMPERIAL
6 small ripe pears
lemon juice
50 g/2 oz sugar
300 ml/½ pint water
100 g/4 oz plain chocolate
knob of butter

AMERICAN
6 small ripe pears
lemon juice
¼ cup sugar
1¼ cups water
4 squares semi-sweet chocolate
nut of butter

Peel the pears, leaving them whole and without removing the stalks. Brush with lemon juice to prevent discoloration.

Dissolve the sugar in the water over a low heat and add the pears. Cook gently for about 20–30 minutes, testing frequently to see if cooked. When cooked but still firm to the touch, carefully remove the pears from the syrup and arrange on a serving dish.

Rapidly boil the remaining syrup until reduced to about 3 tablespoons (U.S. ¼ cup). Break the chocolate into it and stir until the chocolate has melted and the sauce is smooth. Beat in the butter.

Pour the sauce over the pears just before serving. Serve chilled.

Serves 6

VARIATION
In place of the butter add 1 tablespoon double cream to the chocolate sauce.

Pears in wine

Preparation time: 15 minutes
Cooking time: 20–30 minutes (according to the variety and ripeness of the fruit)

METRIC/IMPERIAL
500 ml/17 fl oz red wine
½ lemon, sliced
250 g/9 oz sugar
1 cinnamon stick
freshly grated nutmeg
1 kg/2 lb small firm pears
lemon juice

AMERICAN
2 cups red wine
½ lemon, sliced
1 cup plus 2 tablespoons sugar
1 cinnamon stick
freshly grated nutmeg
2 lb small firm pears
lemon juice

Place the wine, lemon slices, sugar and spices into a stainless saucepan. Heat gently until the sugar has dissolved then bring to the boil.

Peel the pears without removing the stalks. Leave whole if small; if large, halve, quarter and core them. Brush with lemon juice to prevent discoloration.

Place the pears in the boiling syrup. Cover and simmer very slowly, turning the fruit so that it cooks evenly. The cooking time varies greatly according to the variety and ripeness of the pears. Generally allow 20–30 minutes.

When the pears are tender (test with a skewer or pointed knife), drain and arrange on a dish.

Remove the lemon and cinnamon stick from the syrup. Reduce the syrup, watching it carefully. When it coats the back of a spoon, remove from the heat and pour over the pears.

Serve very cold, even chilled.

Serves 6

VARIATIONS
Arrange the pears in wine over a layer of stewed apples.

Fill the centre of a rice or semolina ring with pears in wine.

Normandy pear flan

Preparation time: 25 minutes
Cooking time: 45 minutes
Oven temperature: moderately hot (200°C, 400°F, Gas Mark 6)

METRIC/IMPERIAL
For the pâte brisée:
  illustrated recipe, page 28
300 g/11 oz flour
225 g/8 oz butter
½ teaspoon salt
50 g/2 oz sugar
3–4 tablespoons water
For the filling:
1 kg/2 lb firm ripe pears
6 tablespoons double cream
50 g/2 oz castor sugar
1 liqueur glass kirsch

AMERICAN
For the pâte brisée:
  illustrated recipe, page 28
2¾ cups flour
1 cup butter
½ teaspoon salt
¼ cup sugar
¼–⅓ cup water
For the filling:
2 lb firm ripe pears
½ cup heavy cream
¼ cup sugar
1 liqueur glass kirsch

Make the pâte brisée (see page 28) and leave to stand for 30 minutes.

Line a flan tin 30 cm/12 inches in diameter with the pastry and bake blind in a moderately hot oven for 15 minutes.

Meanwhile peel, halve and core the pears.

Arrange the pears, rounded sides upper-most, in the half-cooked pastry case in a daisy pattern.

Sweeten the cream with the sugar and flavour with the kirsch. Pour over the pears and bake in the oven for 30 minutes.

Serve warm, as it is, or topped with red-currant or raspberry jelly.

Serves 10

Pineapple surprise

Preparation time: 10 minutes, plus 2–3 hours in the refrigerator

METRIC/IMPERIAL
1 pineapple
1 orange
2 bananas
½ grapefruit
2 mandarins or tangerines
125 g/5 oz castor sugar
juice of 1 lemon
1 (483-g/17 fl-oz) block vanilla ice cream

AMERICAN
1 pineapple
1 orange
2 bananas
½ grapefruit
2 tangerines
⅔ cup superfine sugar
juice of 1 lemon
1 pint vanilla ice cream

Cut the pineapple in two lengthways. Cut away the hard centre core and carefully remove the flesh. Keep the skins cool.

Cube the pineapple. Peel the orange, bananas, grapefruit and mandarins.

Cut the bananas into rounds and separate the other fruit into segments. Mix together all the fruit, sprinkle with sugar and lemon juice.

Leave to stand for 2–3 hours in the refrigerator.

Fill the base of the pineapple halves with vanilla ice cream. Fill with fruit and the rest of the ice cream.

Serve immediately.

Serves 6

VARIATIONS
This dessert can be served like a Norwegian omelette. To do so, while the fruit is standing in the refrigerator prepare an Italian meringue.

Place 3 egg whites and 150 g/5 oz (u.s. 1¼ cups) icing sugar in a basin in a bain marie which should not be allowed to boil. Whip over a low heat until the egg white is fluffy and firm.

Place this meringue in an icing bag with a large fluted nozzle and leave until the sweet is ready.

Just before serving preheat the oven to hot (230°C, 450°F, Gas Mark 8). Fill a roasting tin with ice cubes and place the serving dish on them.

Fill the skins which should still be cold with vanilla ice cream and with fruit salad, then using the icing bag cover the top completely with a dome of meringue.

Leave for 2–3 minutes in the hot oven so that the meringue browns without melting the ice cream.

Serve immediately as it is, or warm about 3 tablespoons (u.s. ¼ cup) kirsch, pour over the pineapple halves and flambé.

Carlotta

Preparation time: 45 minutes. Prepare 1 day in advance

METRIC/IMPERIAL
450 g/1 lb strawberries
100 g/4 oz icing sugar
300 ml/½ pint crème Chantilly:
 illustrated recipe, page 25
1 (475-g/1 lb 4-oz) can pineapple rings
 in syrup
32 sponge fingers

AMERICAN
1 lb strawberries
scant cup confectioners' sugar
1¼ cups crème Chantilly:
 illustrated recipe, page 25
1 (20-oz) can pineapple rings in
 syrup
32 lady fingers

Carefully wash the strawberries, drain, dry and hull them. Keep half to one side. Reduce the rest to a purée with a fork or in a liquidiser.

Add the icing sugar to the strawberry purée.

Prepare the crème Chantilly (see page 25).

Mix together the strawberry purée and freshly whipped cream.

Drain the canned pineapple rings and keep the syrup in a shallow dish.

Cover the base of a tin, about 20–23 cm/8–9 inches in diameter, with greaseproof paper. Completely cover the base with pineapple rings.

Cut 16 sponge fingers in half. Quickly dip the flat side into the pineapple syrup. Cover the sides of the tin with the halved sponge fingers placing the rounded sides against the sides of the tin. Cover the pineapple slices with a layer of sponge fingers.

Cut any remaining pineapple into small pieces and add to the strawberry cream. Pour this mixture over the sponge fingers.

Cover completely with sponge fingers (similarly dipped in pineapple syrup), this time placing the flat sides outermost.

Cover with greaseproof paper. Place a plate and a weight over the tin and leave in the refrigerator for 10–12 hours.

Unmould carefully and decorate with strawberries.

Serves 6–8

VARIATION
When strawberries are out of season, make up the recipe with pineapple and double cream. Then decorate the centres of the pineapple rings with glacé cherries and angelica.

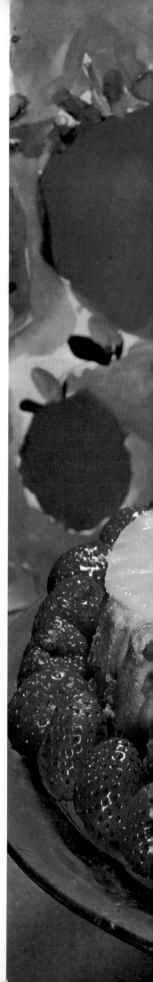

Crêpes Georgette

Preparation and cooking time: 40 minutes-1 hour

METRIC/IMPERIAL
300 ml/½ pint pancake batter:
 illustrated recipe, page 34
12 thin slices fresh pineapple or
 1 (439-g/15½-oz) can pineapple rings
6 tablespoons kirsch
3 tablespoons orange liqueur
about 50 g/2 oz castor sugar
100 g/4 oz butter for cooking
3 tablespoons apricot jam

AMERICAN
1¼ cups pancake batter:
 illustrated recipe, page 34
12 thin slices fresh pineapple or
 1 (15½-oz) can pineapple rings
½ cup kirsch
¼ cup orange liqueur
about ¼ cup superfine sugar
½ cup butter for cooking
¼ cup apricot jam

While the batter is standing, carefully peel the fresh pineapple.

With a serrated knife cut the pineapple into 12 thin rings (5 mm/¼ inch thick at the most). With an apple corer remove the hard centre core. Leave to steep in a shallow dish with the kirsch, orange liqueur and a little sugar. After 1 hour, drain. If using canned pineapple, slice the rings in half or they will be too thick and steep them in kirsch and liqueur, but omit the sugar.

Then cook small pancakes 10–13 cm/ 4–5 inches in diameter. The pancakes

should be quite thin.

When cooked on one side, place a pineapple ring in the centre and cover it with a little batter. Cook gently so that the pancake browns without burning. Turn and cook on the other side.

Keep the pancakes hot and keep separate.

When ready to serve, sprinkle with sugar and serve on hot plates with apricot sauce.

To make the apricot sauce Reduce the jam to a purée and dilute with the kirsch and liqueur in which the pineapple rings were steeped. Heat but do not boil.

Makes 12 small, quite thick pancakes

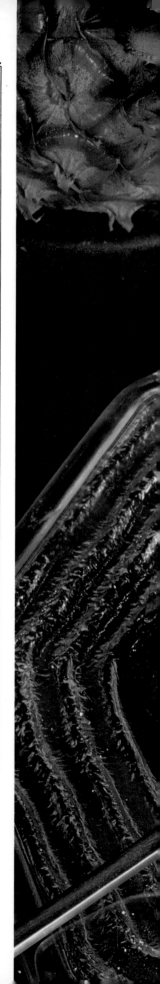

Pineapple cream

**Preparation time: 30 minutes. Prepare 1 day in advance and serve very cold
Cooking time: 30 minutes baking time, plus 7–8 minutes for the caramel
Oven temperature: moderate (180°C, 350°F, Gas Mark 4)**

METRIC/IMPERIAL

For the caramel :
  illustrated recipe, page 38
175 g/6 oz cube sugar
6 tablespoons water
For the cream :
1 (822-g/1 lb 13-oz can) pineapple cubes
  in syrup
75 g/3 oz sugar
6 eggs
2 tablespoons cornflour
3 tablespoons kirsch or rum
Custard: illustrated recipe, page 22

AMERICAN

For the caramel :
  illustrated recipe, page 38
6 oz cube sugar
½ cup water
For the cream :
1 (29-oz) can pineapple cubes in
  syrup
6 tablespoons sugar
6 eggs
3 tablespoons cornstarch
¼ cup kirsch or rum
Custard: illustrated recipe, page 22

Prepare a light caramel in a small saucepan with the cube sugar and water. Pour into a 1.5-litre/2½-pint (U.S. 3-pint) mould and tilt to cover the base and sides.

Reserving the syrup, drain the pineapple cubes and crush in a liquidiser. Place the crushed pineapple, canned syrup and sugar in a saucepan. Boil the mixture for 2–3 minutes, then allow to cool slightly.

Beat the eggs. Add the cornflour (diluting first in a little of the egg to avoid lumps). Pour the warm pineapple mixture into the eggs as for a custard. Flavour with kirsch or rum.

Pour into the caramelised mould. Place the mould in a bain marie and bake in a moderate oven for about 30 minutes.

Leave in the mould until completely cool, then place in the refrigerator.

Turn out of the mould just before serving. Serve with vanilla custard or a custard flavoured with kirsch or rum.

Serves 6–8

Easter gâteau

Preparation time: 45 minutes. Make 1 day in advance
Cooking time: 1 hour
**Oven temperature: moderately hot (200°C, 400°F, Gas Mark 6) reducing
to 190°C, 375°F, Gas Mark 5**

METRIC/IMPERIAL
For the cake:
4 whole eggs
500 g/1 lb 2 oz castor sugar
200 g/7 oz ground almonds
75 g/3 oz flour
100 g/4 oz potato flour
4 egg whites
For the cream:
100 g/4 oz sugar
2 tablespoons water
2 egg yolks
225 g/8 oz unsalted butter
2 tablespoons kirsch
1 (200-g/7-oz) can pineapple pieces in
  syrup
For the decoration:
50 g/2 oz chopped almonds, toasted
various sugars: dark soft brown, icing,
  granulated (about 50 g/2 oz of each)

AMERICAN
For the cake:
4 whole eggs
2¼ cups sugar
scant cup ground almonds
¾ cup flour
⅔ cup potato starch
4 egg whites
For the cream:
½ cup sugar
3 tablespoons water
2 egg yolks
1 cup butter
3 tablespoons kirsch
1 (7-oz) can pineapple pieces in
  syrup
For the decoration:
½ cup chopped toasted almonds
various sugars: dark soft brown,
  confectioners', granulated (about ¼ cup
  of each)

To make the cake Grease a large 28–30 cm/11–12 inch cake tin. Cover the base with greaseproof paper.

In a mixing bowl work the 4 whole eggs into half the sugar until the mixture is white and creamy. Carefully fold in the ground almonds, flour and potato flour.

Whisk the 4 egg whites until stiff, then fold in the remaining sugar.

Carefully fold this meringue into the cake mixture. Pour into the cake tin and cook in a moderately hot oven (200°C, 400°F, Gas Mark 6) for 20 minutes, then reduce the temperature (190°C, 375°F, Gas Mark 5) for the final 40 minutes. If the top of the cake starts to get very dark, cover with a piece of foil during cooking.

To make the pineapple cream Dissolve the sugar in the water. Slowly bring to the boil without stirring. Boil for 2 minutes,

remove from the heat and slowly pour this hot syrup into the egg yolks, whisking continuously. Leave to cool.

Beat the butter until creamy. When the egg and sugar mixture is cool, stir into the butter. Add the kirsch.

Take out enough of the cream to cover the sides of the cake. Finely chop the pineapple and mix into the cream.

To decorate Cut the cake horizontally to give 2 equal rounds. Fill with pineapple cream and replace the top.

Cover the sides thinly with the reserved cream. Coat with the almonds.

Place the cake in the refrigerator and leave for several hours until firm.

Cover the top of the cake with an even layer of brown sugar or finely grated chocolate. Make bell shapes in different sugars with a cardboard stencil.

Serves 16 (halve the quantities to serve 8)

Bird of Paradise

Preparation time: 20 minutes for the cake (prepare 1 day in advance);
 30 minutes for the fruit salad; 15 minutes for the decoration
Cooking time: 25 minutes
Oven temperature: moderately hot (200°C, 400°F, Gas Mark 6)

METRIC/IMPERIAL
1 teaspoon dried yeast
2 tablespoons lukewarm water
150 g/5 oz sugar
3 eggs, separated
150 g/5 oz flour, sifted
125 g/4½ oz butter, melted
grated rind of 1 lemon
For the syrup:
250 ml/8 fl oz water
200 g/7 oz sugar
½ vanilla pod
pinch of cinnamon
juice of 1 lemon
3 tablespoons rum
For the fruit salad:
1 small pineapple
5 oranges
5 bananas
12 glacé cherries

AMERICAN
1 teaspoon active dry yeast
3 tablespoons lukewarm water
⅔ cup sugar
3 eggs, separated
1¼ cups sifted flour
generous ½ cup melted butter
grated rind of 1 lemon
For the syrup:
1 cup water
scant cup sugar
½ vanilla bean
dash of cinnamon
juice of 1 lemon
¼ cup rum
For the fruit salad:
1 small pineapple
5 oranges
5 bananas
12 candied cherries

To make the cake Grease a 1.5-litre/2½-pint (u.s. 3-pint) ring mould. Dissolve the yeast in the water together with ½ teaspoon of the sugar. Leave to stand in a warm place until it is frothy. Beat the egg yolks with the sugar to give a smooth cream. Add the flour and melted butter alternately. Flavour with the grated lemon rind and finally stir in the yeast.

Whisk the egg whites until stiff and fold into the mixture. Pour into the mould and cook in a moderately hot oven for 25 minutes.

Remove from the mould and leave until quite cool.

To make the syrup Boil the water with the sugar, vanilla, cinnamon and lemon juice for 5 minutes. Leave to cool before adding the rum.

To make the fruit salad Cut the pineapple into 1-cm/½-inch slices. Remove the skin and the hard core. Cut the 6 best slices in half and chop the rest into small pieces.

Peel the oranges with a sharp knife, then cut into quarters.

Peel the bananas and cut into 4 or 5 pieces.

Put all the fruit (except the half slices of pineapple which are for decoration) to steep in the rum syrup.

To decorate Place the ring of cake on a large dish and cut into 12 equal portions.

Place a half slice of pineapple between each piece of cake, rounded side uppermost. Form once more into a solid ring.

Inside the ring arrange the fruit salad. Sprinkle with some of the syrup and serve the rest separately.

Decorate each section of cake with a glacé cherry.

Serves 12

Pineapple vacherin

This dessert should be made in 3 stages:
The day before or several hours before the meal, make the ice cream.
1 or 2 hours in advance, make the caramel cubes.
Just before serving, decorate.
Preparation time: 30 minutes for the ice cream, plus 30 minutes for decoration
Setting time: 2–4 hours (depending on the refrigerator)

METRIC/IMPERIAL

1 good size ripe pineapple (about 1 kg/2 lb)
250 g/9 oz icing sugar
150 ml/¼ pint double cream, whipped
For the caramel:
  illustrated recipe, page 38
250 g/9 oz cube sugar
3 tablespoons water
½ teaspoon vinegar
1 prepared meringue case

AMERICAN

1 good size ripe pineapple (about 2 lb)
1 cup plus 2 tablespoons confectioners' sugar
⅔ cup heavy cream, whipped
For the caramel:
  illustrated recipe, page 38
9 oz cube sugar
¼ cup water
½ teaspoon vinegar
1 prepared meringue shell

To make the ice cream Peel the pineapple and cut into thick slices of about 2 cm/¾–1 inch. Remove the hard core, then cut each slice into 8 or 10 even pieces. Keep the best of these pieces (about 20) for decoration.

Reduce the rest to a purée in a liquidiser. Add the icing sugar and whipped cream. Pour into the ice tray of the refrigerator.

Turn to maximum coldness and leave the ice cream until half set. Turn into a very cold bowl and whisk for a few seconds. Refreeze. Repeat this process a second time: this will give an ice cream as frothy as one made in an ice cream maker. Leave the ice cream to set completely.

To make the caramel cubes It is not possible to prepare these more than 1 or 2 hours in advance as the pineapple juice melts the caramel.

Dry the pineapple cubes which were kept to one side when making the ice cream. Place on skewers or metal cocktail sticks (like petits fours which are to be iced).

Prepare a golden brown caramel with the cube sugar, water and vinegar (see page 38).

Quickly dip each pineapple cube into the caramel and leave the pieces to cool on a sheet of foil.

To decorate Just before serving, place the meringue case on a dish. Cut the pineapple ice cream into cubes (it should be very firm) and fill the case with the ice cream cubes.

Arrange the caramel cubes on the ice cream (you can use cocktail sticks for a more pleasing presentation).

Serves 8

Marzipan plum flan

Preparation time: 30 minutes
Cooking time: 50 minutes–1 hour
Oven temperature: moderately hot (200°C, 400°F, Gas Mark 6)

METRIC/IMPERIAL

For the pâte brisée:
  illustrated recipe, page 28
200 g/7 oz flour
100 g/3½ oz butter
½ teaspoon salt
1 tablespoon sugar
3 tablespoons water
For the cream:
1 whole egg
1 egg yolk
100 g/4 oz sugar
50 g/2 oz butter, melted
100 g/4 oz ground almonds
1 tablespoon plum liqueur
For the filling:
1 kg/2 lb small, ripe, well-flavoured
  plums
50 g/2 oz sugar

AMERICAN

For the pâte brisée:
  illustrated recipe, page 28
1¾ cups flour
scant ½ cup butter
½ teaspoon salt
1 tablespoon sugar
¼ cup water
For the cream:
1 whole egg
1 egg yolk
½ cup sugar
¼ cup melted butter
1 cup ground almonds
1 tablespoon plum liqueur
For the filling:
2 lb small, ripe, well-flavored
  plums
¼ cup sugar

Make the pâte brisée (see page 28) and leave to stand for 30 minutes. Line a 28-cm/11-inch flan tin and bake blind in a moderately hot oven for 15–20 minutes.
  Prepare a marzipan cream. Beat the whole egg with the egg yolk and the sugar. When pale and creamy, beat in the melted butter and ground almonds. Flavour with the liqueur.

Spread this cream in the half-cooked pastry case. Wash the plums, halve and stone them. Arrange the plum halves with the cut sides against the cream, overlapping them slightly as they shrink during cooking.
  Sprinkle with 50 g/2 oz (U.S. ¼ cup) sugar. Cook in the moderately hot oven for 30–40 minutes. Serve warm or cold.

Serves 8

NOTE This flan can also be made with quinces, apricots or cherries.

Plum slices

Preparation time: 30 minutes
Cooking time: about 1 hour
Oven temperature: moderately hot (190°C, 375°F, Gas Mark 5)

METRIC/IMPERIAL
175 g/6 oz butter
4 medium-sized eggs
225 g/8 oz sugar
225 g/8 oz flour
1 kg/2 lb plums
1 tablespoon sugar

AMERICAN
¾ cup butter
4 medium-sized eggs
1 cup sugar
2 cups flour
2 lb plums
1 tablespoon sugar

Beat the butter with a spatula until creamy.

Separate the eggs. Add the egg yolks and sugar to the butter and beat well until the mixture is pale and very creamy.

Whisk the egg whites until stiff and beat 2 tablespoons (u.s. 3 tablespoons) into the creamed mixture. Gently fold in the remaining egg white alternately with the flour in small amounts.

Pour the mixture into a greased 23-cm/9-inch square cake tin. Stone and halve the plums and lay them on top of the mixture overlapping slightly to allow for shrinkage during cooking. Sprinkle with sugar.

Cook in a moderately hot oven for about 1 hour.

When the cake is cooked, leave to cool a little before turning out of the tin.

Serves 6–8

Raspberry charlotte

Preparation time: 30 minutes, plus 7-8 hours standing time
Cooking time: 8-10 minutes

METRIC/IMPERIAL	AMERICAN
32 sponge fingers	32 lady fingers
4 tablespoons water	$\frac{1}{3}$ cup water
2 tablespoons raspberry liqueur	3 tablespoons raspberry liqueur
400 g/14 oz raspberries	14 oz raspberries
For the marzipan cream:	*For the marzipan cream:*
250 ml/8 fl oz milk	1 cup milk
$\frac{1}{2}$ vanilla pod, pierced	$\frac{1}{2}$ vanilla bean, pierced
50 g/2 oz sugar	$\frac{1}{4}$ cup sugar
25 g/1 oz flour	$\frac{1}{4}$ cup flour
50 g/2 oz ground almonds	$\frac{1}{2}$ cup ground almonds
1 whole egg	1 whole egg
1 egg yolk	1 egg yolk
raspberries to decorate	raspberries to decorate

First prepare the marzipan cream. Bring the milk to the boil with the vanilla pod. Leave to stand for 10 minutes, then remove the vanilla pod. In a basin mix the sugar, flour and ground almonds. Add the egg (1 whole egg and 1 yolk) and gradually work in the hot vanilla flavoured milk. Bring to the boil, stirring continuously. Allow to bubble 2 or 3 times, remove from the heat and leave to cool.

Dip the sponge fingers lightly in a mixture of water and liqueur and line a charlotte mould with the sugar-coated sides of the sponge fingers against the base and sides of the mould. Break the remaining sponge fingers into pieces.

In the centre spread a layer of marzipan cream, then raspberries, then a few broken sponge fingers. Continue to fill the mould in this way finishing with a layer of sponge fingers. Trim the sponge fingers lining the mould level with the filling and arrange the trimmings on top of the filling.

Press down well and leave to stand in a cool place or refrigerator.

To serve Remove from the mould and surround with raspberries.

Serves 6

NOTE Use raspberry syrup rather than liqueur if this dessert is intended for children.

Carlton figs

Preparation time: 15 minutes

METRIC/IMPERIAL
450 g/1 lb fresh figs
200 g/7 oz raspberries
6 tablespoons double cream, whipped
100 g/4 oz castor sugar

AMERICAN
1 lb fresh figs
7 oz raspberries
½ cup heavy cream, whipped
½ cup superfine sugar

Peel the figs, carefully cut in two and arrange in a fruit bowl. Keep in a cool place.
  Sieve the raspberries to extract the juice.

Add to it the sugar and whipped cream.
  Cover the figs completely with this cream.
  Serve chilled.

Serves 4

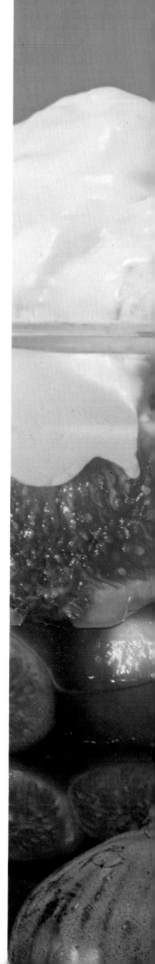

Iced meringues

Preparation time: 20 minutes, plus minimum 2–3 hours freezing at the coldest setting

METRIC/IMPERIAL
350 g/12 oz raspberries
100 g/4 oz icing sugar
6 tablespoons double cream
12 prepared meringue halves

AMERICAN
¾ lb raspberries
scant cup confectioners' sugar
½ cup heavy cream
12 prepared meringue halves

Reserve a few raspberries for the decoration. Reduce the remainder to a purée and add the icing sugar and cream (do not whip).

Pour into ice trays or a shallow container and leave to freeze in the ice-making compartment of the refrigerator or in a freezer (it is not necessary to use an ice cream maker).

To serve Cut the block of ice cream into 12 slices. Place 2 slices between 2 meringues halves, place in a paper case and decorate with the reserved raspberries.

Serves 6

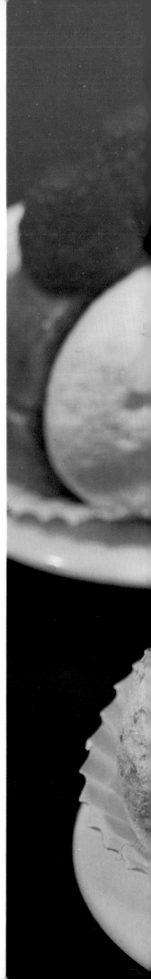

226

Raspberry slices

Preparation time: 10 minutes
Cooking time: 10 minutes

METRIC/IMPERIAL
6 slices stale crusty bread
100 g/4 oz butter
100 g/4 oz castor sugar
225 g/8 oz raspberries
250 ml/8 fl oz double cream
3 tablespoons vanilla sugar

AMERICAN
6 slices stale crusty bread
$\frac{1}{2}$ cup butter
$\frac{1}{2}$ cup sugar
$\frac{1}{2}$ lb raspberries
1 cup heavy cream
$\frac{1}{4}$ cup vanilla sugar

Butter the slices of crusty bread. Cover the buttered sides liberally with sugar.

Melt the rest of the butter in a frying pan over a low heat. Add the prepared slices of bread, sugar sides up.

Cover the pan and cook over a very low heat for about 10 minutes until the sugar has melted. Then remove from the heat and wait until the sugar solidifies to form a crust of icing on each slice of bread.

Cover with raspberries. Mix the cream with the vanilla sugar and serve separately. Everyone can add cream to their bread as they wish.

Serves 6

NOTE This very simple bread recipe can be made with any fruit, particularly with wild berries (blackberries or bilberries).

Raspberry timbale

Preparation time: 30 minutes, plus a minimum of 2 hours freezing

METRIC/IMPERIAL
600 ml/1 pint double cream
250 g/9 oz castor sugar
1 (28-g/1-oz) sachet vanilla sugar
4 large meringue shells
400 g/14 oz raspberries
1 tablespoon kirsch

AMERICAN
2½ cups heavy cream
1 cup plus 2 tablespoons superfine sugar
1 (1-oz) envelope vanilla sugar
4 large meringue shells
14 oz raspberries
1 tablespoon kirsch

Add 1 or 2 crushed ice cubes to the cream to cool and thin it. Add 100 g/4 oz (u.s. ½ cup) of the castor sugar plus the vanilla sugar. Whisk, preferably by hand, until the cream is firm and frothy.

Crush the meringues into rough pieces and carefully mix these pieces into the whipped cream.

Line a charlotte mould with greaseproof paper. Pour the mixture into the mould, pressing down well.

Place in the ice-making compartment of the refrigerator for at least 2–3 hours, or in a freezer.

Meanwhile prepare the raspberries which will accompany the dish. Reserving a few whole raspberries for decoration, steep half the remaining raspberries in the kirsch and 2 tablespoons (u.s. 3 tablespoons) castor sugar. Liquidise the rest of the fruit to a purée, sieve and add the remaining sugar. Heat very slowly until it begins to boil.

Pour this purée over the raspberries in kirsch. Leave to cool then place in the refrigerator.

To serve Turn out the timbale into the centre of the serving dish. Place the reserved whole raspberries around it. Serve with the raspberry sauce.

Serves 6

Celtic tart

Preparation time: 15 minutes
Cooking time: 50 minutes–1 hour
Oven temperature: moderate (160°C, 325°F, Gas Mark 3)

METRIC/IMPERIAL
250 g/9 oz flour, sifted
100 g/4 oz castor sugar
3 eggs, separated
2 tablespoons rum
150 g/5 oz slightly salted butter

AMERICAN
2¼ cups sifted flour
½ cup sugar
3 eggs, separated
3 tablespoons rum
⅔ cup slightly salted butter

Place the flour on a pastry board. Form a well and in it put the sugar, the egg yolks and the rum.

With the fingertips mix first the egg yolks, sugar and rum, gradually working in the flour. When the dough becomes thick, knead in the butter cut into small pieces. Roll the pastry into a ball.

Place in a buttered baking tin 20 cm/ 8 inches in diameter and flatten out with the back of the hand. Smooth the surface. Brush with egg white and decorate with lozenge shapes traced with a fork.

Cook in a moderate oven for 50 minutes– 1 hour.

Serves 6–8

Vanilla ice cream flambé

Preparation time: prepare at least 3-4 hours before serving

METRIC/IMPERIAL
1 litre/1¾ pints vanilla ice cream
225 g/8 oz apricot jam (preferably containing whole fruit)
5 tablespoons (or more) white rum

AMERICAN
1 quart vanilla ice cream
⅔ cup apricot jam (preferably containing whole fruit)
6 tablespoons (or more) white rum

The ice cream should be prepared in advance or bought ready made.

Keep in the refrigerator out of the ice-making compartment for as long as is necessary for it to soften without becoming runny. Remove the ice cream and turn the refrigerator to maximum coldness.

Place about a quarter of the ice cream in a charlotte mould or a 15-cm/6-inch cake tin, pressing down well. Cover with a good spoonful of apricot jam. Add more ice cream, then jam and continue in alternate layers of ice cream and jam, ending with a layer of ice cream.

Place the full mould at once in the ice-making compartment of the refrigerator or in the freezing compartment if you have one. Leave the ice cream to become firm again.

Just before serving, gently heat the rum and turn the ice cream out of the mould. Flambé the rum and pour over the ice cream. Serve at once.

Serves 6

VARIATIONS
Proceed in exactly the same way using different jams and liqueurs:
Strawberries (or raspberries) and kirsch
Blackcurrants and blackcurrant liqueur
Marmalade and curaçao
Pineapple jam and rum
Pear jam and brandy
Prunes, chestnuts, clementines or cherries in spirit with the liquid in which they have been steeped.

Brandy parfait

Preparation time: 8 minutes, plus 1½ hours setting time

METRIC/IMPERIAL
300 ml/½ pint double cream
1 egg yolk
50 g/2 oz icing sugar
6 tablespoons brandy
1 tablespoon vanilla essence

AMERICAN
1¼ cups heavy cream
1 egg yolk
½ cup confectioners' sugar
½ cup brandy
1 tablespoon vanilla extract

Whip the cream until thick. Mix the egg yolk with the icing sugar, brandy and vanilla essence.

Fold the two mixtures together carefully.

Pour into the ice tray of the refrigerator. Place in the ice-making compartment to set or in the freezing compartment if you have one. (It is not essential to use an ice cream maker.)

Serve the parfait turned out on to a napkin, or serve in individual dishes.

Serves 6

Strawberry gâteau

Preparation time: 40 minutes
Cooking time: 35–40 minutes
Oven temperature: moderate (180°C, 350°F, Gas Mark 4)

METRIC/IMPERIAL
8 eggs
200 g/7 oz sugar
150 g/5 oz ground almonds
1 kg/2 lb strawberries
For the crème Chantilly:
  illustrated recipe, page 25
75 g/3 oz icing sugar
1½ (28-g/1-oz) sachets vanilla sugar
450 ml/¾ pint double cream

AMERICAN
8 eggs
scant cup sugar
1¼ cups ground almonds
2 lb strawberries
For the crème Chantilly:
  illustrated recipe, page 25
scant ¾ cup confectioners' sugar
1½ (1-oz) envelopes vanilla sugar
2 cups heavy cream

Separate the eggs. Beat the yolks with the sugar until thick and creamy. Stir in the ground almonds.

Whisk the egg whites until very stiff and fold into the mixture.

Grease two 20-cm/8-inch cake tins and line the base of each with a round of greased greaseproof paper. Divide the mixture between the two tins and spread out evenly.

Bake in a moderate oven for 35–40 minutes. Turn out, remove the greaseproof paper and cool on a cooling tray.

Wash and hull the strawberries. Prepare the crème Chantilly (see page 25) and keep cool.

Slice each cake across into two layers. Place one layer on the serving dish and pipe the crème Chantilly over to completely cover it. Cover with some of the strawberries.

Lay a second layer of cake on the strawberries, cover with more crème Chantilly and strawberries and continue in this way until all four layers of cake are sandwiched together.

Top with a layer of strawberries and piped cream. Keep cool until ready to serve. This dessert should be eaten the same day, but the cake can be made the day before.

Serves 8-10

Strawberry sorbet

Preparation time: 30 minutes, plus 2–3 hours freezing at coldest setting

METRIC/IMPERIAL
450 g/1 lb strawberries
100 g/4 oz castor sugar
1 liqueur glass aniseed liqueur
For the syrup:
200 g/7 oz granulated sugar
300 ml/½ pint water
juice of 3 lemons
grated rind of 1 lemon
For the crème Chantilly:
  illustrated recipe, page 25
25 g/1 oz icing sugar
½ (28-g/1-oz) sachet vanilla sugar
150 ml/¼ pint double cream

AMERICAN
1 lb strawberries
½ cup superfine sugar
1 liqueur glass anise seed liqueur
For the syrup:
scant cup granulated sugar
1¼ cups water
juice of 3 lemons
grated rind of 1 lemon
For the crème Chantilly:
  illustrated recipe, page 25
¼ cup confectioners' sugar
½ (1-oz) envelope vanilla sugar
⅔ cup heavy cream

Wash and hull the strawberries and steep with the castor sugar and the aniseed liqueur.

To make the lemon syrup Dissolve the sugar in the water over low heat then bring to the boil. Add the lemon juice and grated lemon rind. Leave to cool.

Choose 12 good strawberries from those that are steeping and keep for decoration. Purée the rest of the fruit in a liquidiser and add any syrup that may have formed.

Stir together the lemon syrup and strawberry purée. Pour into ice trays or a rigid plastic container and freeze in the ice-making compartment of the refrigerator or in a freezer. The mixture should be whisked thoroughly when semi-frozen and returned to the refrigerator or freezer to freeze.

To serve Fill goblets or fruit dishes with sorbet. Decorate with sweetened crème Chantilly (see page 25) and the reserved strawberries.

Serves 6

Strawberries in vermouth

Preparation time: 10 minutes, plus 2–3 hours chilling time

METRIC/IMPERIAL
1 kg/2 lb strawberries
150 g/5 oz castor sugar
juice of 1 lemon
300 ml/½ pint Pineau des Charentes
    (dry, white vermouth)

AMERICAN
2 lb strawberries
⅔ cup superfine sugar
juice of 1 lemon
1¼ cups Pineau des Charentes
    (dry, white vermouth)

Carefully wash the strawberries, dry and hull. Place in a serving dish, preferably glass. Sprinkle with the castor sugar and lemon juice.

Leave to stand in a cool place for 2–3 hours (or overnight) until the sugar has dissolved. Pour over the vermouth.
    Serve very cold.

Serves 6-8

VARIATIONS
In wine: Steep about 100 g/4 oz of the strawberries in ½ bottle red Bordeaux wine with the juice of 1 orange and 1 small glass brandy. Just before serving, add the sugar and when dissolved add the rest of the strawberries.
In champagne: Steep the strawberries with the sugar and 1 glass chilled champagne or sparkling wine in a salad bowl.

Just before serving, top up with champagne.
In orange: To the prepared, sweetened strawberries add the juice of 3 oranges and 1 liqueur glass orange liqueur. Decorate with slices of orange.
In lemon: Steep the strawberries in sugar using 300 g/11 oz for each kg/2 lb strawberries and the juice of 2 lemons.

Strawberry parfait

Preparation time: 10 minutes, plus 2–3 hours freezing at the coldest setting

METRIC/IMPERIAL
450 g/1 lb strawberries
200 ml/6 fl oz double cream
100 g/4 oz cream cheese
250 g/9 oz icing sugar
For the decoration:
225 g/8 oz strawberries

AMERICAN
1 lb strawberries
$\frac{3}{4}$ cup heavy cream
$\frac{1}{4}$ lb cream cheese
2 cups confectioners' sugar
For the decoration:
$\frac{1}{2}$ lb strawberries

Wash and hull the fruit. Reserve a few good ones for decoration and liquidise the remainder into a purée. Add the cream, cream cheese and icing sugar. Whisk for 2 minutes until the mixture is frothy.

Pour into ice trays and place in the ice-making compartment of the refrigerator or in a freezer. Avoid opening too often during freezing (it is not necessary to use an ice cream maker).

Just before serving turn out of the trays by standing them in cold water for 20 seconds.

Decorate with strawberries which have been reserved for this purpose.

Serves 8–10

VARIATIONS
Strawberry parfait is the most classic of the fruit parfaits but fruits such as black and red currants, raspberries or apricots give equally delicious results. All the fruits are reduced to a purée. If using very acid fruits (such as black or red currants) increase the amount of sugar.

Strawberry flan

Preparation time: 20 minutes
Cooking time: 20-30 minutes to bake blind, plus 35-40 minutes for the filling
Oven temperature: moderately hot (200°C, 400°F, Gas Mark 6)

METRIC/IMPERIAL
For the pâte brisée:
 illustrated recipe, page 28
200 g/7 oz flour
100 g/3½ oz butter
½ teaspoon salt
1 tablespoon sugar
3 tablespoons water
For the filling:
675 g/1½ lb small strawberries
75 g/3 oz sugar

AMERICAN
For the pâte brisée:
 illustrated recipe, page 28
1¾ cups flour
scant ½ cup butter
½ teaspoon salt
1 tablespoon sugar
¼ cup water
For the filling:
1½ lb small strawberries
6 tablespoons sugar

Prepare the pâte brisée (see page 28). Leave to stand for 30 minutes, then roll out and line a 25-cm/10-inch flan tin.

To prevent the pastry rising during cooking, prick the base lightly with a fork and line with greaseproof paper. Fill with baking beans. Cook the flan case blind in a moderately hot oven for 20–30 minutes. Turn out of the tin and leave to cool.

Serves 6

VARIATION
When the pâte brisée has been left to stand, line a flan tin.

Fill the base of the flan with a cream prepared by mixing 2 eggs with 75 g/3 oz (u.s. 6 tablespoons) sugar, a few drops of vanilla essence and 250 ml/8 fl oz (u.s. 1 cup) double cream.

Cook in a moderately hot oven for 35–40 minutes. Check that the pastry base is cooked before removing from the oven.

Wash and hull the strawberries and fill the flan case with the whole fruit, keeping back about 12 strawberries. Purée them and add 75 g/3 oz (u.s. 6 tablespoons) sugar. Warm over a low light until the sugar is completely dissolved.

Pour the syrup over the strawberries to make them shine.

Serve at once.

While the pastry is cooking, wash and hull the strawberries, sprinkle with sugar and leave to stand in a cool place.

When the flan is just warm, arrange the strawberries with their juice on top of the cream. They should be close together. Chill for 1 or 2 hours before serving, so that the strawberry juice can soak into the cream.

Magyar fruit salad

Preparation time: 30 minutes

METRIC/IMPERIAL
225 g/8 oz strawberries
225 g/8 oz cherries
225 g/8 oz apricots
225 g/8 oz peaches
4 tablespoons sugar
6 tablespoons water
1 liqueur glass kirsch or rum

AMERICAN
$\frac{1}{2}$ lb strawberries
$\frac{1}{2}$ lb cherries
$\frac{1}{2}$ lb apricots
$\frac{1}{2}$ lb peaches
$\frac{1}{3}$ cup sugar
$\frac{1}{2}$ cup water
1 liqueur glass kirsch or rum

Wash and hull the strawberries. Wash the cherries, apricots and peaches and remove the stalks. Stone the fruit and cut into pieces if necessary.

Dissolve the sugar in the water over a low heat, then bring to the boil and cook for 1 minute. Pour the boiling syrup over the fruit.

Cover and leave to cool. Keep the fruit salad in the refrigerator, taking care to keep the bowl covered.

Add the liqueur just before serving.

Serves 6

NOTE This recipe is merely an example. All fruits can be used to prepare a fruit salad, either all fresh fruit, or a combination of fresh and canned or frozen fruit.

They can be served in a bowl or in a fruit skin, such as pineapple, orange or grapefruit. Fruits containing little acid should be sprinkled with lemon juice to avoid browning.

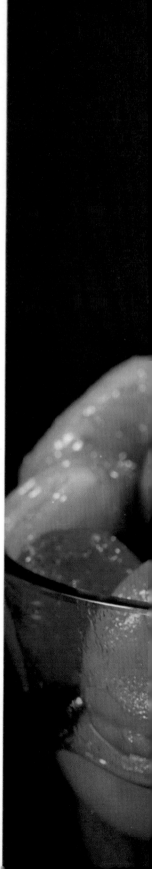

Strawberry semolina

Preparation time: 20 minutes
Cooking time: 20-25 minutes

METRIC/IMPERIAL
500 ml/17 fl oz milk
125 g/4½ oz semolina
200 g/7 oz sugar
pinch of salt
4 egg whites
50 g/2 oz ground almonds
For the strawberry syrup:
350 g/12 oz strawberries (reserve a few
  for decoration)
150 g/5 oz sugar
1 teaspoon lemon juice

AMERICAN
2 cups milk
¾ cup semolina
scant cup sugar
dash of salt
4 egg whites
½ cup ground almonds
For the strawberry syrup:
¾ lb strawberries (reserve a few for
  decoration)
⅔ cup sugar
1 teaspoon lemon juice

Boil the milk. Sprinkle in the semolina and cook for 20 minutes, stirring frequently. Five minutes before it is cooked add the sugar and a pinch of salt.

Whisk the egg whites until stiff.

Remove the semolina from the heat but while still hot mix in the ground almonds and fold in the stiffly beaten egg whites.

Pour into a fluted ring mould which you have rinsed but not wiped and leave to cool.

Wash, hull and crush the strawberries. Cook for 3 minutes with the sugar and lemon juice. Allow to cool.

To serve Remove from the mould while still slightly warm. Decorate with whole strawberries and pour the fresh strawberry syrup around it.

Serves 6

VARIATION
This dish can also be decorated with apricots and accompanied by a sauce prepared in the same way, substituting apricots for strawberries and omitting the lemon juice.